OUR KAMPF

by Michael Gerber and Jonathan Schwarz

Anti-Dedication

To Page Management, the least-understanding landlords a couple of starving writers ever had.

Acknowledgements

Mike and Jon would like to thank the following people for allowing their work to be included in this book: Todd Lynch (art on "The Little Prince" and the *NYREV* parody), Rodger Roundy (art on "Curious George"), and Robert Weisberg (our co-writer on *The Bull Street Journal* project). Cover photo © Darko Novakovic (bigstockphoto.com). Back cover © Skip O'Donnell (istockphoto.com).

 Some material in this book has previously appeared in other forms: p. 9, *The Yale Herald*; pp. 7, 9-13, *The Yale Record*; p. 15, 32, 41, *The New Yorker*; p. 66, *The Atlantic Monthly*; p. 30, *Esquire*; p. 78, *The Wall Street Journal*; p. 95, *The New York Times*; pp. 39, 51, 56, *Seattle Weekly*; pp. 36, 69, 76, *The Village Voice*. The authors would like to thank all those publications for allowing them to eat occasionally during this period in their lives.

This book has been pointedly ignored by the Library of Congress.

Table of Contents

And Then Everything Went Crazy

Still Alive? *Yes!*

A Few Choice Words...

Dear Friend:

As you read *Our Kampf*, we hope you will feel one emotion above all others: gratitude. Gratitude that you are only reading this book, as opposed to having the contents recited to you, in a soundproofed basement somewhere in the vast Gacy-land that is suburban Chicago. "First, it puts the lotion on its skin, then it quiets down because this next paragraph is really funny."

Had we abducted you, it would've been nothing personal; we were simply that desperate to communicate. Of course, during the years we wrote this material, we weren't exactly sure what we wanted to say, or how. We might have just as easily written arias as 750-word humor pieces. The only thing we did know was that—like that scene in Alien—there was something inside us that just had to come out. And as in that scene, getting it out hurt us much more than it could ever possibly hurt you.

We expect your experience of life will resonate with ours: that the world is at once genuinely terrifying and winningly silly, with both aspects getting more so all the time. In any case, with this book we feel Part I of our nameless mission is complete.[*] However, the mission continues, and we hope you'll visit us online at mikegerber.com (Mike) and tinyrevolution.com (Jon). Let us know about your own nameless mission, and what you thought of *Our Kampf*.

Whether you contact us or not, we believe in some sense we'll already know. Partly because everything in the universe is connected by a gossamer latticework of invisible vibrations. And partly because we're attached by suction cups to the ceiling of the room you're sitting in right now.[†]

—Mike & Jon
December 2006

Comments? Questions? Want to make this book the central text of your new religion?
ourkampf@tinyrevolution.com

---

[*] "The true mission is always nameless. To name it is to doom it...to alert the enemy."—*Church of the Subgenius*

[†] DON'T LOOK UP

A Few Choice Words

A Few Choice Words

My Friend

La Presidente

Jon
The Yale Record
October 1989

"I'm just a normal teenager," says 15-year-old Christy Snowden of Santa Monica, California, as she flops onto her pink-comforter covered bed. And indeed, her bedroom (on the second floor of her family's home in a serene, affluent suburban development) would seem to indicate just that. The walls are covered with posters of her heroines and heartthrobs: Debbie Gibson, Sigorney Weaver, and Mary Lou Retton in the former category, Terence Trent D'Arby, Jon Bon Jovi ("He's *so* cute"), and Bruce Springsteen in the latter. Her closets are filled with clothes perfectly attuned to the whims of adolescent fashion. A high school biology textbook lies open on her desk, and pictures of her two best friends, Terri and Cindy, are tucked into the corners of her mirror. Yes, Christy Snowden would seem to be the most normal of teenagers, except for one thing—on March 17th, Christy will be sworn in as the 56th President of the tiny, strife-torn Central American nation of Guatemala.

"My parents have always told me that I could anything if I put my mind to it," says Christ with her impish, infectious smile. "And as long as I can remember this has been all I've wanted to do." The Snowden family is sitting together in their comfortable, tastefully decorated living room (at least Christy and her parents are—her six-year-old brother Billy is in and out, tearing around the house with a new model airplane), discussing Christy's rise to power. Arthur Snowden is an optometrist, and Carol works as a paralegal in downtown Santa Monica; neither is surprised by what their daughter has accomplished.

"It all started the Christmas when she was five," says her father. "That morning she came and woke us up at the crack of dawn. My first thought was that she had gotten impatient and wanted to start opening presents. Instead, she looked me straight in the eye and said, 'Daddy, I'm going to be President of Guatemala.'"

Christy laughs. "I don't even *remember* that."

"At the time, of course, Arthur and I just smiled," says Carol Snowden. "We thought it was the cutest thing. But as she got older, we realized she was serious."

"Who knows where she got the idea," says Arthur. "Maybe from something she saw on television. But pretty soon there was just no stopping her. The big question now is where she got the talent for this—certainly not from my side of the family."

"Well, dear, that's not completely true," says Carol. "Wasn't your cousin John vice-president of his high school?"

The phone rings in the kitchen, and Christy jumps up to answer it. After a few minutes she returns, looking glum. "That was Terri," she says. "Cindy and her are going to a movie. But I have to stay here and wait for a call from the head of my transition team."

This brings up the subject of the effect that Christy's ambitions have had on her life outside of the political arena. What has been the reaction of the other students at Santa Monica High to her election? "Well, my friends all think it's pretty neat," says Christy. "But a lot of people that don't really know me think that I just did it to get into college." She laughs. "Of course, some of them never paid attention in the first place—a couple of people congratulated me on being elected President of Peru!" Her commitment to her dreams has also kept her from being as social as she might be otherwise—for instance, she's never had a serious boyfriend. She has a lot of male friends, she says, "but I think they get kind of intimidated. I mean, I try to explain that Guatemala isn't that geopolitically important, but guys my age just don't like going out with heads of state."

One area that Christy has refused to compromise, however, has been academics. She has been going to a private tutor for the last year and a half to make up for the time she has had to spend out of school, either traveling in Central America, or raising money for her campaign, and she has no plans to stop after her inauguration. "I know an education is really important," she says. "I mean, I'm not going to be President of Guatemala my whole life. I have to have something to fall back on—I don't want to end up endorsing products, like General Megia." After her five year term is over, she plans to major in economics at an American university and then hopefully get a job in the banking industry. Of course, many teenagers in her position would say much the same thing, but Christy's commitment to her education is genuine; the day before the elections, for instance, she flew home to take a test in algebra. She charmingly makes light of this, however, saying "I just couldn't miss it—Mr. Davidson's make-ups are killers!" Christ obviously looks back happily on her two years of high school, and says that she only has one regret: "I kind of wish now that I hadn't stopped taking Spanish. But I guess that's all water under the bridge."

The phone rings again and Christy runs to get it. With her out of the room, her parents talk more openly about what Christy's political career looks like from their point of view. "You should have seen her when she got the call that Cerezo had conceded," says Carol. "She was just walking on air. Then she even got a congratulatory call from President Reagan. Pretty heady stuff for a girl who doesn't even have her driver's license!" She smiles. "Now parents come up to us at parties and ask, 'How can we make sure that *our* child is the President of Guatemala too? What's the secret?'"

But although Arthur and Carol are obviously proud of Christy, as the conversation continues it becomes evident that they see a darker side to her achievements. What do they think of their daughter taking office in a country with a long history of brutal military rule, where assassinations and coups d'etat are the order of the day?

"Well, I think she's growing up too fast," says Arthur.

"Now, dear," says Carol, patting his knee. "I'm sure all parents think that about their children." But it is evident that she is concerned as well. "I don't know," she continues. "I just want this to be a positive experience for her. Especially at this age, it would be so easy for her to get hurt."

They also worry about the effect that Christy's presidency will have on Billy. Although up to now his interests have always lain in different directions, they are afraid that he may now suddenly feel that he has to compete with her.

"I just don't want him to think he has to top her by getting elected President of Brazil or something like that," says Arthur. "There are lots of other areas in which he can excel. But I know that he doesn't want people to always think of him as 'the brother of the President.'"

In the end, however, Christy's parents know that they will have to trust her to use her own best judgment. "She's gong to have an eleven o'clock curfew, of course," says Carol, "but we're not going to get involved in running the government unless she asks us to. After all, she's the president. You know, I think that she's always kind of worried about what we think about all this, but we told her, 'As long as you're happy, we're happy.'"

By the time Christy returns to the living room, Billy has settled on the couch next to his mother, and Arthur Snowden is leaving to buy milk for the next morning's breakfast. Christy asks if he will also pick up some soda and potato chips for her party the coming weekend.

"Well, I will if I can, dear," he says, "I don't want to have to go to the automatic teller machine for more money."

"You better, Dad," replies Christy, "or when I'm sworn in, I'll throw you in a tiny, stinking, vermin-infested prison cell!"

The entire family laughs; it is a longstanding joke between them. Christy rushes to hug her father, and in that moment it becomes clear that she truly is an ordinary teenager—an ordinary teenager who just happens to be the President-elect of the most populous nation in Central America. □

Dear *Yale Record*,
Life is difficult for us of the phylum *Phylatia Luthus*. We live only a scant 32 minutes, during which time we must mate, give birth, and write a short letter to the publication of our choice.

Appolonia Milicent Thraft

Jon
The Yale Record
October 1989

The Little Prince

Mike
Yale Herald
September 1989
(illustrations by
Todd Lynch)

Come over here, I want to tell U a story. I had crashed my aeroplane in Africa (in the region called the Sahara) and was starting 2 repair the engine when a little man in a purple cape and spike heels came up 2 me. He introduced himself as "Prince" and politely asked me if I could draw him a guitar. When I told him that I couldn't draw, and that I hadn't drawn anything but boa constrictors since I was six, he replied that he didn't care, and politely asked me again. So I tried, and even though I didn't like it, Prince said that he was very pleased and asked if I could draw him an amplifier as well. As I was busily doing this, he started writhing around on the sand composing a song called "Kiss" which went on 2 reach number one on the Black and Pop charts, as well as sell over three million copies worldwide.

"Where do U come from?" I asked him, finishing the amplifier.

He pointed up in2 the sky. "Do U see that planet there?"

I nodded yes, even though the hot desert sun had nearly blinded me. "Well, that's Minnesota."

As he looked up at the planet, Prince said that he had a purple house. "Is that all that is on your planet?" I asked. "No, no," he said, and gave a little piping laugh as he did the splits, then launched in2 a feedback-drenched solo. (I had not realized I had given him a fuzzbox on the amplifier I had drawn, but I had.) "I have a massive recording studio, and a couple of BMWs, and lots of girlfriends." Prince was now licking the neck of his guitar. I winced, and he said, "You're just like all the other grownups." He looked hurt, and started 2 walk away.

"Where R U going?" I was alarmed, forgetting that this was Prince, and not just a lost little boy. For he stood only five foot three inches tall, even in his spike

heeled boots. His chemically treated curls bounced in the wind and he came back, just like nothing had happened.

"R U in2 God? I am," said Prince, and proceeded to tell me about a woman named Sheila E. She wore fishnet stockings and lingerie and nearly nothing else. "She must get cold," I said, turning back 2 my broken engine. "No, man, she's hot—but I'm going out with Sheena Easton now," he added, and ran a calloused fingertip over his pencil-thin cheesy moustache.

"I made some movies, once," said Prince, and pounded out an intricate polyrhythm on the wreckage of my plane which made me want to get up and shake my thang. "Were they good?" I asked, once the urge 2 groove had passed. "One of them was, and one of them wasn't," he said, looking up at the sky again.

"I have 2 go back," he said, and absent-mindedly pulled up his shirt, exposing a nearly hairless chest and a brace of healthy nipples. I asked him 2 stay, for I had become quite attached to the little Prince, even in the short time that I had known him.

"NO! I am very reclusive and besides I want 2 ride my big purple motorcycle and want 2 make about twenty records in a week. Besides, I think Madonna is going to finally return some of my phone calls." He set his little face sternly and I knew that I could not convince him to stay.

"But could you draw one more thing before I go?" he asked. I immediately said yes, and drew him this:

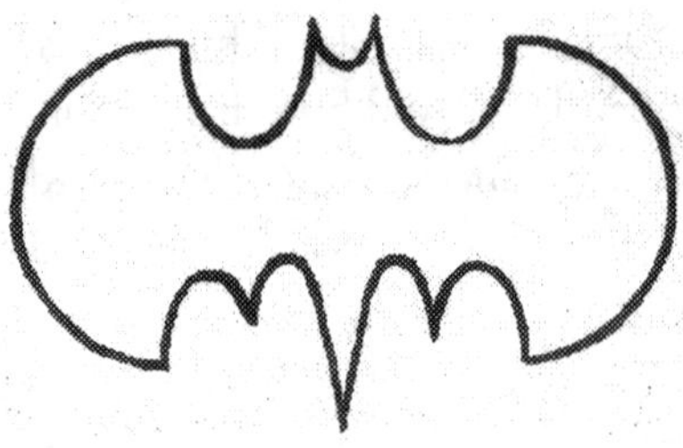

His little elfin sexy face lit up with joy when he saw the drawing. "If I can hook in2 this, I could make a mint! Two weeks in the studio, sample Jack Nicholson's voice a few times, and voila! I don't even have to sing, not really!" With that, he bid me goodbye, and disappeared over a sand dune.

Now, whenever I look toward the stars at night, I hear a little sexy voice screaming, "Get your funk up!" I know he's up there somewhere, and I can hear him laughing. All the way to the bank. □

Jon
The Yale Record
January 1990

Dear *Yale Record,*
Say what you like about ice fishing or good times with good friends—for my money, there's nothing more fun than going down to the zoo and feeding pennies to the seals.

Noam Randall
Utica, NY

The Lost Quotations of Chairman Mao

Mike
The Yale Record
February 1991

"Boys don't make passes at girls who are fascist."

—from "Nice Proletarian Girls Do"
speech delivered June 14, 1963

"When you assume, you make an ass out of you, and of me. Not to mention the Party, and *that's* a no-no."

—from "The Next Thing I Say Will Be False,"
speech delivered October 25, 1957

"It is helpful to think of China as a big, big bus. At Shanghai, 17,234,000 people get on, and 23, 618 get off. At Canton, 5,987,000 get on, and 5 people get off. At Beijing, 4,887 people get on, and 2,436,000 get off. Now: who is the driver?

I'm the driver. *Mao's* the driver."

—from "Rules of the Road,"
speech delivered May 5, 1950

"Never freeze mayonnaise. You'll get an oily mess."

—from "Eat to Win,"
informal talk delivered at
Chinese Communist Party kegger
23 March, 1961

"Every neighborhood—every one—has a kid who likes to put firecrackers up a cat's butt. I was that kid."

—from "It's Mao-tastic!"
TV movie dramatizing
the Chairman's life aired
November 30, 1973

"Look—if you push on a fish's eye, it's mouth opens! 'Hello Comrade Zhao! I am your dinner, I am going to bite your nose off!' Heh, heh."

—cutting up with Zhao Enlai
Party Congress cookout
mid-1971

"There's a monster in my pants, and he does a little dance. Like so."

—from Mao's censored
apppearance on
American Bandstand,
September 17, 1957

"I have only worn lipstick once in my life, and I was drunk."

—overheard at a Shaanxi clambake,
July 20, 1953

"There are two armies in China; one to fight, and one to do little chores. No! Don't laugh! Have you ever seen an entire battalion clean an oven?"

—from remarks before the Third Annual
Beijing Rodeo/Tractor Pull,
October 2, 1972

"My bowels are acting up. Let's have a purge."

—from "An Evening With Mao,"
unaired PBS special taped
June 13, 1966

"We do not fear the imperialist running dogs and their minions. We do not fear their atomic and hydrogen bombs; if attacked, all of China shall stand upon a chair, and, when given the signal, jump off simultaneously. This is the technology of the proletariat. And believe you me, it will *kick your ass.*"

—from "It is a Good Thing for an Enemy to Attack,
Rather Than Just Sit There and Make Fun of You"
Pep talk delivered at CCP Bake Sale,
February 7, 1971 □

Jon
The Yale Record
December 1989

Dear *Yale Record,*
Take me out to the ballgame, take me out to the crowd. Buy me some peanuts and Cracker Jack, then clean it up after I get carsick and vomit on the way home.

Your Seven-Year-Old
Nephew

Jon
The Yale Record
December 1989

Dear Sirs,
Did you know that fireflies crawl to the top of their blade of grass at dusk every night in order to effectively signal a mate? That's why I *always* mow the lawn at 8:30.

Jim

Curious George Gets Sold For Medical Experiments

Mike (with excellent art by Rodger Roundy) • *The Yale Record* • October 1989

1. George lived with the man in the yellow hat, who brought him from the jungle many years ago.

2. The man in the yellow hat needed money. He was drinking a lot, and playing something called "the numbers." A big, hairy man named Mario was going to come and break his kneecaps with a ball-peen hamme.

3. One day, the man in the yellow hat saw an ad in the newspaper. Then he and George drove in his car to Lederle Labs.

4. As soon as they got there, George was shot with a dart gun.

5. When George woke up, he was in a little cage. The man in the yellow hat was gone, but there was a man in a white lab coat. George was very unhappy until he noticed all the other monkeys around. Then he felt better.

6. The man in the white coat gave George food and things to look at. George particularly enjoyed the copy of "Lusty, Lusty, Big 'n' Busty" that he grabbed when the man wasn't looking.

7. *One morning, George was let out of his cage. "Today we are going to do an experiment," said the man. "Get in this box." George was excited. This would be fun!*

8. *But it wasn't! Every so often, the box shocked George and he couldn't get out. The man in the white coat was writing something, and ignored his screeching.*

9. *When they let George out, he was very drpressed. George was also mad at the man in the yllow hat for selling him! What a fink! George thought.*

10. *After tranquilizing George to make him more docile, the man took him to the operating room "Great!" thought George,. "Maybe I'll finally get a real nose instead of just two holes in may face."*

11. *But when George woke up, his nose was the same. He was very hungry, though, and ate 346 bananas for lunch.*

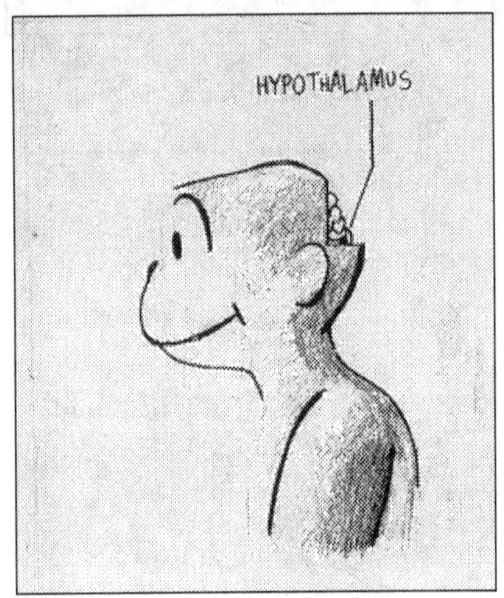

12. *You see, the man in the white coat had removed George's hypothalamus, that part of the brain which regulates food intake. Of course, scientists have known this fact for years, but there is no harm in being sure.*

13. *So George ate and ate, and even started eating his bedclothes when—POP!—his stomach exploded. Too bad!*

14. *Meanwhile, the man in the yellow hat was snaring another unsuspecting victim...* □

What We Talk About When We Talk About Doughnuts

Jon
The New Yorker
written June 1988, published May 10, 1999

My friend Jim Forrer was talking. Jim Forrer is a professional fish measurer, and sometimes that gives him the right.

We were sitting around the kitchen table drinking gin and smoking. There was Jim and me and his wife, Elizabeth—Lisa, we called her, or sometimes Frank—and my wife, Carol.

There was a bowl of peanuts sitting on the table, but nobody ate many of them, because we were drinking and smoking. We were talking to ourselves like this: Some of us are drinking more than we are smoking, and some of us are smoking more than we are drinking. Some of us are drinking and smoking about the same amount.

We went on drinking and smoking for a while, and somehow we got on the subject of doughnuts. Jim thought that real doughnuts were nothing less than spiritual doughnuts. He said he had spent ten minutes at a seminary before he had gone to fish-measuring school. He said he still looked back on those minutes as the most important minutes of his life.

Lisa said that the man she lived with before Jim had really liked doughnuts. She said he liked them so much that sometimes he would shoot at them with his gun, or flush them down the toilet. Sometimes he would put them on the living-room rug, climb up on the coffee table, and jump off directly on top of them. Then, she said, he would dress them up in little doughnut clothes and eat them and pretend they were screaming in agony.

"It was scary," she said.

Carol and I smiled at each other.

Just then I dropped a peanut on the floor. It rolled behind the refrigerator. It was hard to get it out. It was very hard. But not so hard as other things. Other things had been harder.

"I like doughnuts as much as anyone," said Jim. He took a sip of his drink. "I like them at breakfast, and sometimes lunch."

"Now, hon, you know that's not true," said Lisa.

"What do you mean?" said Jim. "I eat doughnuts a lot."

"No, you don't," said Lisa. "And I've never seen you eat a doughnut at lunch."

"Has it ever occurred to you once in your goddam life that I might not tell you every time I eat a goddam dougnut? Has that ever occurred to you once?" said Jim. *"Christ."* He mimed strangling her, hitting her in the head with a pickaxe, and strafing her with machinegun fire.

He took a sip from his drink, and then stopped, so he could smoke.

Jim's dog was scratching at the door, but we couldn't let him out. We were drinking and smoking.

When I met Jim, he was still married to Nancy, his forty-five wife. They had been very much in love, but one day she inhaled too much helium and just floated away. Then he met Lisa.

When I introduced Jim to Carol he said she was a real person. I was glad, because my college girlfriend, Hillary, was a facsimile person. She was warm and loving, and with the proper equipment could be sent across the country in seconds. But things didn't work out.

"Has anyone ever seen a really big doughnut?" said Carol. "I did once. At a pawnshop in Maine." She paused. But then she didn't said anything afterwards, so actually it was less like a pause and more like a full stop.

"No," said Jim, taking a sip of his drink, "but I ate some miniature doughnuts once." He took a sip of the gin he was drinking. "I ate ten or twelve of them." Jim leaned back, rubbed his temples, and took a sip from his glass. "I thought," he said, pausing to take a sip of his drink, "that they were pretty," he continued, sipping from his drink, "good." Jim took one last sip, this time of my drink.

We reminisced about the best doughnuts we had had in our lives.

"The best doughnut I ever had," said Jim, "was when I was working for Harry Niven. Do you remember Harry, honey?"

"Of course," said Lisa.

"Compared to him I can't measure a fish at all," said Jim. "I mean, there was a man who could measure a fish!"

"But you're very good," said Lisa. "Now that Harry's gone, you're the best there is."

"No, I'm not," said Jim. "I've never been any good at all. I hate myself." Jim took a pencil and stuck it about four inches up his nose.

"Ouch," he said. "I've punctured my brain."

We went on talking.

"The best doughnut I ever had," said Lisa, "was when I was dating Daniel." We all knew about Daniel. They had been deeply in love and on the brink of marriage when Lisa realized that he was a hologram.

"Hold on a second, hon," Carol said to Lisa. She turned to me. "Do you want to get divorced?"

"O.K.," I said.

Carol and I left and got divorced. Then we came back with our new spouses, Dave and Terri.

We all sat there talking, the six of us in the dark. We went on talking and talking, even after the gin ran out. Talking about doughnuts. Talking about doughnuts in the dark. □

Sketch: "Bad Parents"

Jon
from The Yale Record Show
April 1991

(<u>OPEN ON</u>: INT. BEDROOM OF DANNY, AN 11 YEAR-OLD BOY. DANNY IS WORKING AT HIS DESK AS HIS DAD KNOCKS ON THE OPEN DOOR AND STICKS HIS HEAD IN.)

DAD

Daniel? Can your mother and I come in and talk to you?

DANNY

Sure, dad. Hi, Mom.

(THEY ENTER AND SIT DOWN)

I just finished my homework. Mrs. Denby says I'm really good at math!

MOM

That's great, honey.

(PAUSE)

DANNY

So, what did you want to talk to me about?

MOM

Well, Danny, now that you're eleven, pretty soon you'll be starting puberty, so your Dad and I want to be sure you understand what's going to be happening to you.

DANNY

Oh, Mom, I know about all that!

DAD

Maybe you do and maybe you don't, Daniel. It's awfully to easy to hear rumors about this stuff from other kids your age, so we just want to be sure that you get the right information. Now... soon your body is going to be changing, and you're probably doing to start thinking a lot about girls, which is why the first thing I want us to discuss is masturbation.

DANNY

(embarrassed)

Dad...

DAD

Danny, masturbation is nothing to be embarrassed about. It's perfectly normal. Doing it won't make you go blind, or grow hair on your palms.

DANNY

Yeah, I know...

DAD

Pretty much the only thing you do want to be careful of, if you do it too much your penis will fall off and you'll turn into a girl.

DANNY

Really?

MOM

Oh, you bet – that's what happened to me!

DANNY

That didn't tell us about that in school...

DAD

Really? That's surprising...I wonder what else they didn't tell you. You know about sperm, and the number of sperm that each man has?

DANNY

No...how many sperm does a man have?

DAD

Each man has three. So if you ever want to have children of your own, you should think about conserving them.

DANNY

Wow.

MOM

Uh-huh. Your Dad didn't plan ahead, and now you're an only child.

DAD

Now, I assume you know something about actual intercourse. Are there any questions you want to ask about it?

DANNY

Uh, well, in school they talk about condoms all the time –

MOM

Oh, forget about condoms!

DANNY

But what about the girl getting pregnant, and diseases?

MOM

Don't worry about that – it'll never happen to you. Beside, you know what they say – sex with a condom is like taking a shower in a raincoat.

DANNY

But –

MOM

No, no. Skin on skin – that's the only way to go.

DAD

Anything else?

DANNY

Uh, Jimmy's parents have this book that keeps on talking about something called "fellatio." He told me what it was, but – well, what is it?

DAD

Oh, that's an easy one. Fellatio is a small town outside Venice, in Italy. Now, when I was your age, what I really wanted to know was what was going on with girls at the same time all these things were happening to me. Do you have any questions you want to ask about that?

DANNY

Well, I've heard a lot of girls in my class talking about getting their periods, and I guess I understanding what that means, but why does it happen?

MOM

Well, Danny, women menstruate for two reasons: first of all, because every month a lining builds up in the uterus so it can support a fertilized egg. Then if the egg isn't fertilized, the lining has to be shed. And secondly, because women are evil.

DAD

Yes, women are evil – and <u>unclean</u>.

MOM

Now, another thing you may be wondering about is whether or not vaginas have teeth. Well, let me put your mind to rest on that – they don't. Because technically they're not teeth at all, they're more like those things whales have to strain plankton.

DAD

They are razor sharp, though, so watch out!

MOM

We also want you to know that if you like a girl, and she likes you, but for some reason things don't work out, you don't have to feel like a failure. It's sad, but sometimes that happens with adults, even when they love each other very much.

DANNY

Uh-huh. Billy told me in school that his parents are getting divorced. But he said they were always yelling at him, and he thinks it's his fault.

DAD

Billy thinks it's <u>his</u> fault?

DANNY

Uh-huh.

DAD

Wow, he's smarter than I thought. 95% of all divorces are exclusively the fault of the children.

DANNY

They are?

MOM

You bet! Remember when you spilled your juice in the car last week? Your father and I came this close to breaking up because of that.

DAD

Well, Danny, I hope this talk helped clear some things up for you.

DANNY

Uh...yeah, I guess. Look, I got an A on my math test today.

DAD

Hmm. That's nice. But you shouldn't waste your time working hard in school, son.

DANNY

I shouldn't?

DAD

No, of course not. I mean, you like to play sports, right?

DANNY

Uh-huh.

DAD

Then you'll be a professional athlete. And they don't need to know anything about math.

MOM

All right, young man. It's quarter of – I want you asleep in that bed by ten.

DANNY

Okay.

DAD

Good. I hope you remember what we talked about tonight, and that if you ever have any questions about anything, you can always come to us. We just want you to have the right information so you can make your own decisions about these things. Now...I saw on the news that there are a lot of vampires in this area tonight. I locked the windows, so they probably won't be able to get in. (BEAT) On the other hand, of course, you never know. Goodnight.

MOM
(blowing him a kiss)

Sweet dreams.

(THEY EXIT)

(OUT) □

Mike
(GREAT
illustrations by
Todd Lynch)
unpublished
28pp parody
1994-95

PARODY!

Garry Wills Versus George F. Will in a Test of Wills

Th*N*w Y*rk R*vi*w of B**ks

$4.25
CAN. $6.35

ASIMOV: THE THINKING MAN'S SEX GOD

PARODY!

Steven J. Gould on the Forgotten Science of Mixology

Th*\ N*w Y*rk R*vi*w

of Bks**

$4.25
CAN. $6.35

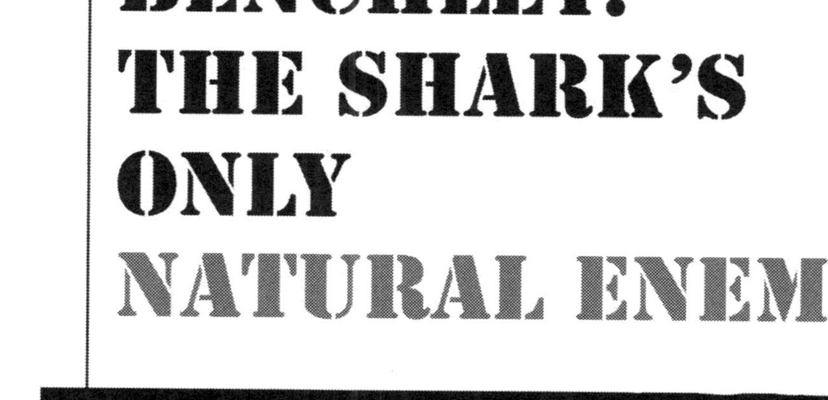

BENCHLEY: THE SHARK'S ONLY NATURAL ENEMY

Material from Puck Magazine

Sometime during his senior year, Mike came up with a fascinating scheme: what if there was a magazine that collected all the best material from the college humor magazines across the country? And what if that magazine was inserted inside college newspapers? And what if a kid who had just graduated college, had no money, and no real experience in the publishing business, spent about 18 months of his life trying to start that magazine?

Mike
Puck
Fall 1992

This was clearly an idea whose time had come…in about 1925. And just in case anybody didn't already know how old-fashioned the idea was, Mike decided to call it *PUCK*, after the legendary humor publication popular in the 1870s. Because there's nothing that excites today's youth more than a humor magazine from the Presidency of Rutherford B. Hayes.

Actually, the idea wasn't as crazy as it sounded—in 1991, the internet did not exist, and advertisers had been reduced to loitering on college campuses in funny costumes, handing out disposable razors in hopes of luring lifetime customers. The only thing between *PUCK* becoming the next *National Lampoon* was about $5,000,000 in start-up capital.

PUCK was Mike's first project after graduation, and represented his determination to do exactly what he wanted to do, bills be damned. This endeavor ended predictably—in a personal and financial collapse—but it proved that Mike was a person who was going places. And wasn't afraid to drag others down with him.

Our Statement of Principles

1. *PUCK* shall at all times strive to improve its readers by running material that is nourishing to the mind, body and spirit. (The "body" is defined as everything up to but **not** including the breasts, thighs, buttocks and bikini area.)
2. *PUCK* will not encourage antisocial or illegal behaviors, and when such acts are necessary for "artistic purposes", they will be shown to lead inevitably to poverty, disease and death.
3. *PUCK* will show respect for its elders, regardless of the propriety, wisdom or charity of their actions.
4. *PUCK* will not make light of the misfortunes of others, even though we both know that they deserved it.
5. *PUCK* will strive to be even-handed, except where the personal grudges of the Editors come into play.
6. *PUCK* will not show pictures of dead bodies at any time, ever. Except on page 19.

The Last Thoughts of JFK

Now *that's* a brunette.
Wo-oah! Nice cans.
Oh, Daddy like! *Daddy like!*
Hey, Red! Does the carpet match the drapes?
Boy, she sure has a fine—
ow
ow
ow
ow
Wait'll I get my hands on Lynd— □

CIGAR
Asphyxionado

WINSTON CHURCHILL:
TINY PENIS?

THIRTEEN CIGARS TO AVOID

STOGIES OF THE GODS?

THE VIRGIN MARTINI

THE VIOLENT WORLD OF WORMFIGHTING

0 73361 64909 6

Mike • *unpublished parody proposal* • October 1995

THE BULL STREET JOURNAL

HIGHLY UNAUTHORIZED PARODY

Wipeout

Clinton Injures Pride, Arm, Ankle and Face in Street Luge Mishap

Bizarre Attempt to Capture Still More Votes Goes Awry; President All Messed Up

The Campaign Continues?

BY JOSIAH BARTLETT
Staff Reporter of THE BULL STREET JOURNAL

SEATTLE—President Clinton broke his right arm and left ankle today while attempting to "street luge," or roll down a hill while lying on a small wheeled board, in a bohemian neighborhood near downtown Seattle. The Chief Executive was airlifted to a nearby hospital, where he was treated for his injuries, including facial contusions. He is expected to be released tomorrow. Though none of these injuries were life-threatening, they did force President Clinton to cancel a later speaking engagement at Seattle's famous Pike Place Market, the place where they throw the fish.

"He slid under a car," said a witness. "His face looks like hamburger—it'll look even worse when it scabs up." Bystanders said that Clinton was bellowing as he rolled down a hill, lying on the special board used in this unconventional sport. Two Secret Service agents were powerless to prevent the Chief Executive from losing control and sliding under a parked Toyota, striking it at approximately 2:32 p.m. Pacific Standard Time. At impact, radar guns clocked the President at 27 miles per hour.

President Clinton

President Clinton had just finished

What's New?—

* * *

Business and Finance

FEDERAL RESERVE Board Chair Alan Greenspan announced today that he is stepping down from his post, effective immediately, so that he may have his head frozen. The 63-year-old will be placed in suspended animation until the U.S. economy becomes more predictable, placid and prosperous. "Three thousand years seems about right," said Greenspan. "I figured, why fight it? 'Nighty-night!'"

(Article on Page A2)

* * *

Mitsubishi has renamed its 1997 Eclipse midsized sedan the "Mitsubishi Dragon-Which-Devours-the-Sun," in an effort to woo the growing number of car buyers who reject science in favor of the tenets of arcane non-Western hoodoo.

(Article on Page B1)

* * *

In a victory for Microsoft, as well as other American high-tech firms, a Washington district court has ruled that torture and brainwashing are "legal enough" treatment for industrial spies. The plantiff, Raymond Skittle, was caught prowling around the company's Redmond, Washington, campus and subjected to several days of "emphatic physical persuasion" last October. Skittle, now earless, plans to appeal.

(Article on Page A3)

* * *

The FAA is set to announce that it will allow airliners to do tricks during domestic flights. "We'll let them do barrel rolls first," said a spokesperson. "Then, if nobody crashes, we'll let passengers jitterbug on the wings."

* * *

Bakster Healing executives, in an effort to force Daly to the bargaining table, have hidden the keys to Daly's Pensacola headquarters. "We keep calling those rats, and they won't tell us where they buried them," a disgruntled Daly official said. "My dog's locked in there, and he's probably crapping all over the place."

* * *

World-Wide

With the United States owing over $1 billion in back dues to the United Nations, Secretary-General Boutros Boutros-Boutros announced that the New York–based organization may attempt to evict the U.S. from the rest of the country. "We have sent them letters, we have suspended them from use of the swimming pool—in other words, we've tried to be cordial about it," he said in a speech to the UN General Assembly yesterday. "Now, no more Mr. Nice World-Peace Organization."

* * *

A UN human-rights official said Japan should pay damages to the 200,000 women it forced into prostitution during World War II. Japan snorted and said that they would, if the UN official did it first. (See Related Article on page B2.)

Meanwhile, Amnesty International said that they "didn't see what was so funny" about using slave labor in the illegal CD factories currently dotting mainland China. Chinese officials replied that the Chinese sense of humor is quite subtle and pointed to their recent "invitation to the world to test its nuclear weapons on Taiwan" as an example.

* * *

The latest record from new age synth noodler Yanni, a collection of Japanese corporate anthems, has surpassed Michael Jackson's *Thriller* as the biggest seller in the history of that Yanni-crazed isle. Other artists are rushing to record company anthems, or make up new ones; Bruce Springsteen has reportedly accepted over $45 million to craft a tune for Matsushita.

* * *

Minister Louis Farrakhan, head of the Nation of Islam, announced that his organization was releasing a new cologne, "Atonement. . .for Men." The scent, test-marketed by Libya's feared Ministry of Fragrance, uses sandalwood, musk notes and just a hint of ammonia to, in Farrakhan's words, "evoke the distinctive tang of the atoning man."

* * *

Financial bigwig Felix Rohatyn admitted that he cannot read or write. "Nor can I see or smell, but I can add and subtract with the best of 'em," he said in a press release. The 63-year-old hopes to encourage illiterates in the banking and investment communities to come forward and seek help. "It gudd he do," said an industry analyst. (Article on Page A2.)

* * *

Use of Graphs in *Bull Street Journal*

(More Graphs on Page C1.)

Please Pass the Catnip: Feline Stock Whiz Confounds Experts, Self

* * *

Dopey Owner is Now Sixth Richest Woman in US; What's the Cat's Secret?

BY WM. WHIPPLE
Staff Reporter of THE BULL STREET JOURNAL

AMPERSAND, Ohio—Every day, at 5:30 a.m., the 3,000 people camped outside Mrs. Eudora Limpet's modest two-bedroom Victorian home in Ampersand, Ohio, wake up, hoping to catch a glimpse of a miracle that defies all scientific explanations. Millions more, from every part of the world, are provided with up-to-the minute reports of events inside 1133 Happy Tree Lane in this tiny Midwestern hamlet.

You see, at about this time, Mrs. Limpet's tabby cat Pepper arises and begins moving about the house. And stock markets from Tokyo to Caracas tremble in anticipation. Because, as Mr. Louis

Eudora Limpet & Pepper

Washington Wire

An Especially Weak Report From The Bull Street Journal's Capital Bureau

EX-LABOR SECRETARY Robert Reich announces that unemployment has dropped to -84%.

The sudden surge is due to changes in the way employment is measured, ordered by Secretary Reich in July, shortly after he was struck by lightning while waterskiing. Changes include counting all pets as being employed and reclassifying most human activities as jobs. "For instance, I have thirty-one jobs," explained Reich.

The Republican leadership in the Congress calls the report "non-election-year voodoo," and plans to counter with a report of their own, demonstrating that no one in the United States has held a job since fiscal year 1962.

President Clinton is promising, in his second term to cut the death rate by 75%—"and even more for kids."

THE DEPARTMENT OF Agriculture unveils new regulations governing the number of insect parts in food packaged for human consumption.

A surprise is the change in how many grasshopper heads are allowed in a pound of corn meal: from seven heads to ten billion. "It's obvious they bowed to political pressure," says one disgruntled Agriculture employee. "The grasshopper head lobby is

Nobody Home!

Webster Technologies Downsizes Itself Into Strategic Extinction

Stock Price Rises 117%

'No One Left to Fire'

BY ROBT TREAT PAINE
Staff Reporter of THE BULL STREET JOURNAL

CHARLOTTE—Alan Roosevelt pulls a small trash can from under a secretary's desk, which is immaculate. The can is empty, but he takes out the clear plastic liner anyway, and replaces it with a new one. "Soft gig. Creeps me out, though," Roosevelt laughs nervously and looks around the room, which is brightly-lit, with no signs of recent activity. "We gotta do it anyway. Otherwise the dust would build up." He laughs again; the only other sound is the soft whir of the air conditioning. In the next room, a fly vainly tries to beat its way out of a closed window. A tumbleweed scurries by, riding the lonesome breeze.

No One

This is the stark North Carolina headquarters of Webster Technologies, a water-purification company perched on the leading edge of this cutthroat, ever-changing business. Thanks to its innovative use of ordinary household colanders, it enjoyed two decades of solid profitability, before falling on hard times in the late 1980s. Vigorous, vocal stockholder angst over the company's poor performance resulted in an kamikazoid restructuring plan; since 1991, the company has been making steady, if painful, progress towards its twin goals of paring staff down

Mike & Jon (with add'l material by Rob Weisberg) • *self-published* • January 1997 a short impromptu speech at Caffe Roma, a local coffeehouse frequented by tattoo artisans, students, and people of uncertain employment. As he posed "pulling a latte" for photographers, he spied some local youth "street luging" on the hill outside. Apparently in an effort to energize the well-caffeinated but still-indolent crowd, off he went.

Onlookers said that Clinton had some difficulty convincing the youngsters to let him try. "You know, I was rebellious when I was younger, just like you." Clinton then donned a wool cap sporting the emblem "Wu Tang", but the young *slackier* remained unimpressed until the President revealed his pierced nipple, a souveneir from Oxford.

Street luge, an urban cousin of the Olympic event, is one of several so-called "extreme sports" popular with today's youth and glamorized by frequent exposure on MTV and ESPN, two cult cable channels. James Lofton, of the Washington, D.C.–based Brookings Institute, said, "Extreme sports are essentially the suicide attempt reborn as recreation." He added that most extreme sports involve equipment "originally created for the space program, and nearly as expensive."

Political observers saw the President's painful stunt as an attempt to continue his successful 1996 campaign—throughout his entire second term "or longer, if necessary." Among 18- to 24-year-olds, the President finished a worrisome second, behind perennial fourth- or fifth-party candidate Lenora Fulani "because she has a cool name."

However, the cynical denizens of Seattle's Capitol Hill neighborhood, the veritable cradle of slackerdom, were unimpressed by Clinton's attempt. "He looked stiff on the board, like a mounted fish," said "The Remora," a freelance hemp merchant and sometime student at Cornish College of the Arts, just up the road from the crash site. "If he grew a soul patch [a variant of goatee nesting between

Please Turn to Page A8, Column 1

NASA announced that the microorganisms discovered on a Martian meteor perished as a result of a heavy tax burden coupled with a bloated, meddlesome bureaucracy. "Let it be a lesson to us all," said Dr. Wayne Aspirin, Chief Economist for NASA. Aspirin would not comment on whether markets free enough to sustain life exist outside this solar system.

* * *

In a controversial move, the Federal Reserve Board plans to cut the lending rate to zero today in an effort to spur a lagging economy. "Go to it, fellas!" read a press release to be issued this morning. "Last one to 30% growth is a rotten egg!"

* * *

A group of former editors are suing their ex-boss, Time-Life, style maven Martha Stuart. The suit, asking for damages of $50 million, says that Ms. Stuart caused "grave psychological damage" by holding editorial meetings while defecating. "Ahh, everybody does that," said Reginald Bismuth-Lewis, a spokesperson for Ms. Stuart.

* * *

Markets—

Stocks: Volume 7 shares. Dow Jones Industrials 6050.04 up 982. Hurrah!

Bonds: Lehman Brothers Treasury index 14.05, off 1023. (*Whew.* If you're in bonds, go have a drink on the Club car.)

Commodities: Baby Oil $1.49 a pint, up .003. Dow Jones futures index 175.43 up 2. Dow Jones grasshopper head futures index 12012.52, up 11030.

Dollar: three Hershey kisses and a dollar equals 100 yen, up from two M&Ms; 1900 pesos and a Mexican toddler, up from a bird.

The embattled Edison Project announced "a last-ditch effort to get kids interested in history"—a hyper-violent video game called *Live Free or DIE!* This game pits great figures from American history against each other in a futuristic, kung-fu flavored fight to the death. CEO Benno Schmidt, once an educational figure of some importance, delighted the press by demonstrating how William Jennings Bryan can rip an opponent's spine out "by force of oratory alone!"

* * *

Frenchy scientists announced that common species of spiders wear hats, and the usually-sleepy American haberdashery industry is abuzz. "We could get 400 cowboy hats from a single piece of felt," said Giacomo Stetson, of Stetson Hats. "Some of our salespeople are a little squeamish," said a spokesperson for Kangol, "but we feel that after the training program, they'll realize that spiders are just like anybody else." (Article on Page B1.)

* * *

The latest Beltway bombshell is—believe it or not—a slavery scandal. When 500 Washington politicians, lobbyists and journalists were surveyed by recent Gallup poll, 62% of them agreed with the statement, "I own slaves." "Frankly, I think they're all sitting on a political volcano," said one insider. Columnist George Will, owner of Matthew, Karen, and James, disagrees. "I guess slavery is no longer *politically correct*," he snorted. "The American people have always been envious of their masters, and of me in particular."

* * *

The American Association of Editors released new guidelines on the identification of sources. From now on "off the record" will mean that the person being quoted was whispering, and sources quoted "on deep background" will have to stand behind reporters when they talk.

Grimm, a broker with Golden Sacs in San Francisco, says. "This cat is the greatest financial genius since Adam Smith. Possibly greater."

Pepper picks stocks. And Pepper, it seems, has never made a mistake. Ever.

How can an animal with an estimated IQ of 29 outperform the Dow Jones by 3,152 percent over a five-year period? Mrs. Limpet, herself no genius, is at a loss to explain it all. "Pepper was a perfectly normal cat — yarn, mice, milk, hairballs, the usual. Maybe even on the dim side — he never could even figure out the toy mouse I bought him years ago. But one day, I had spread out some stock certificates on the kitchen table — my eyesight isn't what it used to be, and I had mistaken them for playing cards — when he jumped up, sat down on one and wouldn't get up."

What the kindly old Mrs. Limpet didn't know is that her feline had taken his morning nap on 50 shares of Flapjack Pharmaceuticals, which was that very day to become the takeover target of British leveraged-buyout artist Sir Buckminster Squeam (Squeam has since filed a $39 million lawsuit against Pepper, claiming the kitty had inside knowledge of his planned takeover. "Said animal had probably spoken to Mr. Squeam's feline Monroe in an illegal attempt to subvert the world financial system," he has claimed in a deposition filed in London).

When the white-haired septuagenarian mentioned Pepper's behavior in passing

Please Turn to Page A3, Column 5

... stronger than you think." The Department is also promulgating peculiar new standards where none existed before, including nine praying mantis legs per hamburger, one-half boll weevil per walnut, and seven hundred scorpions per orange.

Grasshopper head futures at the Chicago Board of Trade skyrocketed nearly 4,000% yesterday.

MONEY TALKS in Washington, but something else talks even louder: backrubs.

"It's well known that Dick Gephardt will vote any way you want if you have 'the talented hands,'" said one lobbyist. "He rubs up against you like a cat and purrs." But love of the rub knows no party: GOP honcho Richard Armey is rumored to have changed a recent vote because the Saudi ambassador came over to his house the night before to rub his back.

The backrub craze has created new opportunities for lobbyists. If a legislator wakes up in the middle of the night with a bad dream, Lockheed lobbyists will let congressmen sleep in their beds with them, and will even sing them "Kumbaya"; most shocking, representatives of embattled Archer Daniel Midlands sometimes write them notes so that they can stay home from Congress—*even if they're not really sick.*

DOG DAYS: Undersecretary of State for East Asia Franklin Emory sparked controversy yesterday by suggesting the U.S. should declare war on China "because they eat puppy dogs." In a speech at Harvard University, Emory said that "China is currently laying plans to invade the United States and seize our rich canine resources. ...Pretty soon old Deng will be stretched out on Venice Beach looking at the ladies and eating Lassie a la King."

Secretary of State Madeline Albright quickly disavowed Emory's speech.

"What really gets my blood boiling," stated Albright, *"is the Persians. They use their hand to wipe their butt!"*

A CIA OFFICIAL said that Bill Clinton has been a victim of mindcontrol since 1995. "A rogue element of the VFW abducted the President after a speech in Omaha, and re-programmed his brain to act like a Republican." Since the brainwashed "Nebraskan Candidate" won handily, "we assume that the plan backfired." The White House said Clinton has no plans to seek therapy for his condition. "If it ain't broke, don't fix it—anyway, HRC likes it."

to the bone, and squeezing the absolute maximum efficiency from its physical plant.

The complete lack of activity, which lends a slightly ghost town-like feeling to offices which once bustled, would make one believe that Webster was a company on the ropes. Not so — its stock, listed on the Nasdaq, has posted a 230% rise since June, on the strength of massive employee layoffs. So massive, in fact, that there is no one left to run the company.

The final straw, "the final piece in the puzzle," came yesterday, when Webster CEO Neil F. Jordan, who had presided over the company's efforts to regain profitability, summarily fired President Quinn Daloit, and, in a brutal bit of business harikiri, himself. "...and don't come back!" He told himself in a press release.

Webster's stock leaped at the news that the company had voluntarily imploded. As of yesterday's close, Webster Technology's stock stood at 78 3/4, up 117% from the previous day's trading. It remains to be seen whether this immediate proof of Jordan's acumen will solidify into permanent gains for Webster, but most observers are confident. "There's no one there," said an industry executive. "Who's gonna do anything?"

"In the past, Webster was in a lot of businesses we shouldn't have been in, like water-purification," said Jordan, in a statement released yesterday afternoon. "Over the past several years, we here at Webster have worked hard to scale back, to concentrate on only those areas where we can compete effectively. The question is: what can Webster do best? And the answer is: nothing. *Absolutely nothing.*

"Through spit, grit, and hard work, we have reached our goal. Goodbye."

Competitors have taken notice of Webster's meteoric rise. Daniel Grady, President of BTI, Webster's main competitor, said, "For years, we've been playing the fool for Webster's schemes — they'd lay off twenty or so people, we'd hire them and expand our operations. Meanwhile, we were having a harder and harder time keeping up." BTI has been steadily losing market share to Webster as the latter bled itself white; the two companies have abruptly switched places, when BTI had a commanding 64% share as late as May 1994, before Webster's lemming-like plan began in earnest. After yesterday's coup de grace, rumors

Please Tu n to Page A3, Column 6

TODAY'S CONTENTS

SORRY IT'S SMALL—WE'VE BEEN SICK

DEAD BODIES: Corpses, long considered useless and icky, have proven to be a source of profit, profit, PROFIT! **Page B1.**

MEDICINE: Lilly scientists reveal that addition of Prozac makes plants grow sideways, **A4**.

WHO'S NEWS: CEO, after a brush with death, finds family overrated, more fulfillment in work, **B2**.

PUBLISHING: Recent deluge of parodies render normal magazines meaningless, **B3**.

POLITICS & POLICY: Bizarre loophole in regulation makes cows, bees fill out tax forms, **A8**.

INTERNATIONAL: China announces plans to stick a fiber-optic cable in back of every citizen's head, **B4**.

LEISURE & ARTS: "Poop Dreams," guano documentary, is reviewed, **A5**.

FOREIGN MARKETS: Nikkei plummets due to South Korean curse, **C2**.

We wanted to include more (there are 20 pages of it!) but the type was just too tiny.

Lunch With J. Robert Oppenheimer

Mike
Esquire
November 1999

Eccentricity has always been an accepted prerogative of brilliance. We expect, maybe even demand, that our geniuses be weirdoes; stumbling through life chafed by normalcy seems the proper cosmic counterbalance to their gifts.

Some quirks are well known: Einstein's five identical suits, for example (freed from wondering what to wear each morning, he could ponder the Universe). Others are obscure: James Joyce's fear of ink caused him to write the epochal Dubliners in beet-juice. So, to illustrate -- and celebrate -- the eccentricities of the truly gifted, we have compiled the following assortment of vignettes, culled from a variety of sources.

Orson Welles

dramatist, filmmaker

"Orson was given to peculiar passions. For example, he loved The Who. I know he never forgave Ken Russell for not giving him the lead in "Tommy.'" Imagine what he could've done with that!

He only saw The Who play once—in Cincinnati, when those people got crushed. There wasn't a stampede; what happened was some idiots tried to pick Orson up and pass him towards the stage over their heads. The first few could do it, but there was this little guy who couldn't. Orson lost his balance and mashed several people. The press covered it up, but Orson felt terrible; his corpulence had turned him into a weapon.

He still had a sense of humor about it, though. When he met Pete Townshend several years afterward, he said, in that marvelous voice of his, 'Pete, you never had a bigger fan.'"—Peter Bogdanovich, from the 1987 documentary "Io, Orsonalia!"

Miles Davis

Musician

"From the time he was a little boy, Miles was different. For one thing, he wore his underpants backwards, and did his business out the fly. Did that all his life far as I know. He'd find his way, and stick to it, and the person who tried to get him to change, watch out!

I remember the day we got him his first trumpet. He was six, and his daddy won it in a church raffle. Mr. Davis had no interest in music, and no time besides, so he gave it to Miles. It was love at first sight. Miles did everything with that trumpet in his mouth — talked, ate, swore. Some kids at school made fun of him for it, but Miles cut 'em with a straight razor. [laughs] That shut 'em up quick."—Cleota Henry Davis, from "Momma Miles," an interview in *Rolling Stone*, 2/16/71.

Benjamin Franklin

Printer, publisher, statesman, inventor

"Inventions poured from Franklin throughout his life. Some of "Ben's brainstorms" are still in use today: the Franklin stove, the wind chime, bifocals. Publisher of the first magazine in America, he was the father of the 'blow-in' card and the centerfold. He also ran the first public relations agency, acting as a flack for the whale-oil industry.

Unfortunately, one of Franklin's less-fortunate ideas nearly drove him from the public arena. In 1767, he created "Franklin's Roto-stimulator," a bulky, cast-iron contraption apparently powered by lightning. Franklin believed it would encourage milk production in cows, which it did, most powerfully.

Not surprisingly, the device began to be used as a marital aid—the contraption's hefty caresses proved too vigorous for all but the sturdiest Founding Mothers. Still, "Franklin's Roto-stimulator" grew in popularity, until in 1779 an improperly-grounded Delaware woman was electrified in the throes of ecstasy. As the inventor, Franklin was liable. It took all of his connections and diplomatic skills to avoid prison. Speaking in front of the Continental Congress he said, 'Gentlemen, grant me this: at least she died happy.' The chamber exploded in laughter, and after that the danger was passed."—Scott Towson, from *Creepy Tales From American History*, Scholastic Books, page 324 ff.

Ernest Hemingway

Writer

"From about 1919, Hemingway was afflicted by constant intestinal gas, the power or pungency of which no medicine could assuage; doctors now believe it was a nervous condition brought on by the War, or some canapés served by Gertrude Stein. For the next 40 years, Papa struggled against his 'damned gastric breezes,' forced into a solitary career interspersed with outdoor activity.

Spain he loved, for the Spanish culture is indulgent to flatulence. They would not hold a fragrant burst against a man—in fact, bullfighters considered one's wind a potent weapon against the charging beast. Many of them owed their lives to the few seconds a lifted leg could grant in the face of a pain-addled brute.

In the end, Hemingway was defeated, as we all are, by the limitations of the body. His suicide note reads: "I must have relief from this dreadful stench of my own making." —from *A Taste of Papa*, J. H. Johnsen, Scribner's, 1965.

J. Robert Oppenheimer

Physicist

"Einstein was there, too; he shambled in looking like, in Kitty Oppenheimer's words, 'some alter kocker who sings to the mangoes at the grocery.' He greeted me warmly, and showed me some complicated breakdancing moves he had just picked up from the great mathematician John Von Neumann. We all danced at Los Alamos; it relieved the tension.

We sat down to lunch. I was astonished to see that Oppie was drinking blue paint—filled with lead and surely poisonous! I sprang up and tried to knock the glass from his hand, but he fended me off, saying bitterly, "The government says I'm too smart for my own good, so I'm making myself stupider. Lead paint tastes sweet, you know — try some." It was a sad coda to his Senate ordeal the year before, where his security clearance was removed in disgrace.

Oppenheimer kept to this bizarre regimen until his death; soon after our lunch, he forgot about the number 'three' entirely, which rendered his later work useless. It was a tragedy."—from *Thunderpussy: My Life in Physics*, by Enrico Fermi, Harper and Row, 1973, page 393.

Jean Genet

Writer, dramatist

"But the final straw came when little Jean, a fourth-grader, was put in charge of the school's Christmas play. The work, loosely based on the Magi story but now hinging on Genet's obsession with the powerful thighs and buttocks of the Christ child, was filled full of buggery, larceny and prostitution of the basest kind. The audience, mostly parents and siblings, were utterly appalled, unaware that they were witnessing the first work of one of this century's premier dramatists. The school paper, *La Boche*, was kinder: "M. Genet's `The

Kings' is a challenging work, which plunges the audience into a symbolic landscape of loneliness, scatology, and erotic despair."

The administration did not see it that way. Jean was sent to Mettray Reform School less than 24 hours after the curtain came down."—from *Forever Genet,* by Marie-Christophe Lanacaine, Aurole and Company Publishers, Paris, 1987, page 107.

Bob Dylan

musician, poet

"Now, see, the true story of the bike crash is this. Only a few people know this. Bobby got some yohimbe, and was mixing it with gin, which anybody who was alive back then will tell you is a dangerous combo. Anyway, he and Robbie [Robertson] and I were just sitting around and all of the sudden he gets this jones, you know, to '[make love to] a denizen of the forest.' He was in no condition to drive or anything, so he crashed and messed himself up real bad.

So then the doctors had to replace all this stuff: an arm, both legs, part of his nose, and lip. Luckily for Bobby they had learned a lot from Vietnam; five years earlier and he would've been finished. Nobody likes a singer who looks like bloody scrambled eggs. So that war did one good thing at least! [laughs] Since then, Bobby's been mostly mechanical. 'Dylan goes electric', right? He owes his career to prosthetics, and trick photography. If you listen real close you can hear the gears and wheels inside him.

He joked about it. Listen to that Royal Albert Hall bootleg, during "It Ain't Me, Babe,": 'I'm not me, babe/No, no, no, I'm not me, babe/I'm a frizzy-haired cyborg, babe.' ...Me and Robbie are the only ones who knows what he meant."—Vince Quivey, from "Road Hogs: Interviews With Rock's Most Legendary Roadies," CD-ROM from Voyager, 1995. □

From the Desk of Larry Summers

Mike & Jon
The New Yorker
July 12, 1999

Just between you and me, shouldn't the World Bank be encouraging MORE migration of the dirty industries to the [Less Developed Countries]? A given amount of health-impairing pollution should be done in the country with the lowest cost... I think the economic logic behind dumping a load of toxic waste in the lowest-wage country is impeccable and we should face up to that."—December 1991 memo by Larry Summers, then chief economist for the World Bank.

"Folks:

Thanks for your warm welcome last Friday. I must admit that I hate karaoke, but Bob Reich's version of "Stone Free" is something I'll remember for a long time. ;) As I said then, my door is always open, and I want to hear any bright ideas you have. Remember, there are no stupid answers.

To start the flow, here's a brainstorm I had this morning: just between you and me, shouldn't we be encouraging pharmacutical companies to test their RISKIEST new products on the people of the Third World? Sure, the incarcerated are a good half-step, especially those who can't read well enough to understand the release form. But even some crank-head who killed his girlfriend over a lottery ticket is going to get out someday, and have some job dealing fro-yo at the mall. Then he'll be pulling down the American minimum wage, money that a Hmong tribesman wouldn't make if he lived to be a thousand. So it would be much more economically efficient to dose Zapatistas and Uzbekistani yak hearders with Merck's newest anti-baldness/impotence/prostate enlargement cream. Squirt it from cropdusters, or just dump it in the water supply. Frankly, these people's lives are so awful that even horrible side effects would be an improvement. We should face up to that."—**July 31, 1999**

"...Just between you and me, wouldn't it make more economic sense if companies doing business in Less Developed Nations could BUY their workers' rights? Like, the right to strike? Or to criticize the company? Or to go to the bathroom? Right now these people make so little money that they (or their parents) would be glad to accept a small lump sum, in return for which they would give up their right not to be chained to the machinery. They wouldn't even miss it...The companies would get an orderly workforce legally forbidden from doing anything but work, and their employees would get perhaps USD$5.00. Both sides benefit! This is what free trade is all about, and we should face up to that!"—**January 14, 2000**

"...Just between you and me, there's only one way we're ever going to colonize the moon: Third World labor. Lots of it. And let's face it, there's going to be an INCREDIBLE rate of mortality, especially if we use that cheap, shoddy material for the spacesuits (see my previous memo, "Cutting Corners in Outer Space"). On the good side, life expectancy in the LDCs is already pitifully low, particularly now that enormous loads of toxic waste have been dumped there. "Listen, Champ, you're going to be dying soon anyway, so why not do it on the moon, with some money in your pocket!" We'd get so many applicants that we'd have to run some kind of lottery, possibly on the Internet. (Al Gore loves this angle.)

As always, keep your eyes out for the leaker—unfortunately, the cleaning service checks out. Plus, I know you just started facing up to this Moon idea, but I just had a brainstorm about what to do with all those extra children in Ireland."—**May 20, 2000** ☐

Thirty Things We HATE About Hell

Mike & Jon
written 1999, published in the anthology *101 Damnations* 2002

1. It's *really* cliquey.
2. You get this weird vibe from Satan if you joke about him being in that *South Park* movie, like he thinks he's a big star or something.
3. The black flies out by the Lake of Everlasting Fire; those little bastards BITE!
4. Mother Theresa will *not* stop bitching about how her paperwork got messed up. Cry me a river, Terry—down here, *everybody's* innocent.
5. No ESPN. C'mon—that's part of basic cable!
6. The snotty emails you get from your friends in Heaven. They always talk about how great it is, then feel bad and say something like, "Like everywhere, it's not perfect."
7. The Salisbury Steak in the dining halls.
8. The rumor is, Nasdaq is considering delisting our shares (HLL, dump 'em if you got

'em). This after, "If you come here instead of Purgatory, I'll give you stock options." Boy, he really *is* the Lord of Lies.
9. All the models here are soooo dumb.
10. It's impossible to get a cab. Well, not *impossible,* but you have to wait forever, especially when it's raining.
11. Disembowelment. The old saying is full of shit—it hurts *every* time they do it.
12. I've gotten Jeffrey Dahmer as my Secret Santa for three straight years.
13. SAT Thursdays.
14. All the bragging. Guys, it's Hell—if you were really all that, you wouldn't be here.
15. No pets, can you believe it? Satan says he's allergic, but I think he does it just to torment us.
16. The architecture. They tore down all those beautiful medieval buildings! They redid Circles Five through Nine in the early Seventies, and now they look like some crummy community college.
17. The mail service is the *worst.* I haven't gotten a magazine with an unripped cover in 500 years. If you complain, they just look at you with this bored expression.
18. All the movies are second-run, so you hear the endings from the new arrivals before you can see it. Totally ruined that "Bruce Willis is a ghost" movie for me.
19. The demons all have this "unholier-than-thou" attitude.
20. Everybody's plastic surgery is voided when they get here. Yikes.
21. All the tourists looking for Dante. He's not *HERE,* idiots!
22. Everybody underdresses for everything. Would it kill you to wear something besides a T-shirt and cut offs, once in a while? This is Hell, not California.
23. My obnoxious six-hundred and sixty-six roommates. Wash a dish once in an eternty, would you? I'm not your mother! (She's over in the women's dorm.)
24. Everybody is so religious. That boat's left the dock, folks.
25. Hitler. You're not funny, dude, so stop trying.
26. The variable sales tax. You can never tell what anything's going to cost, so you never have enough money when you get to the cashier. I haven't been able to buy anything for years.
27. Listening to everyone argue, "Which is worse, the liquid gold enemas or the brain-eating worms?" Can we just agree they both suck, and leave it at that!
28. Every year the Devil rereads *Paradise Lost* and pulls the ol' "drink-and-dial." What a loser.
29. Whenever the Incendio-Demons set Pol Pot on fire, somebody always yells, "Hey, do you smell Pot?" It wasn't funny the first 20,000 times, wiseass.
30. My bunkmate Jean-Paul Sartre keeps mumbling "I was right. I was so, *so* right." □

Mike
Weekend Update
1998

Officials say many buildings in London's West End are being severely eroded by people urinating on them. Meanwhile, experts have determined that Manhattan island was once the size of South America.

Jon
Weekend Update
2001

The US-China spy plane standoff has become the first for-eign policy crisis of the Bush presidency. Sources say W has sought counsel from his father on how to deal with conflicts in Asia. The former president had urged his son to meet personally with China's leadership—then vomit on them.

Mike
Weekend Update
2001

A Harvard Medical School study has determined that rectal thermometers are still the best way to take a baby's temperature. Plus, it really teaches the baby who's boss.

WNPR AM910 • "Your Public Radio Station"	
5 am	**Sound Money.** Silicon Valley's growing Amish community; three ex-SDSers turned venture-cap moguls; The Body Shop's Anita Rodderick on how to make "mad loot" while retaining that all-important sense of moral superiority.
6 am	**Living on Earth.** Electric power from burning junk mail; the Founding Fathers and hemp; solar-powered cell phones. Plus: frogs everywhere are dying and YOU are responsible.
7-10 am	**Morning Edition.** Incredibly alarming things that happened while you were asleep, quietly presented; Greenspan's inflation worries, day 10,003; today's birthdays: Ken Kesey is 80, Billie Jean King is 64, Jann Wenner is 59.
10 am - Noon	**On the Line.** (call in show) Today's topic: "Imagining a Feminist Pornography." Scheduled guests include the obligatory Susie Bright; Michael Lerner, editor of *Tikkun*; and former First Lady Barbara Bush. Then, on Listener Soapbox: "Are parents who *don't* drive Volvos irresponsible?"
Noon - 2 pm	**New York and Company.** (call in show) Author of new book, *Punny Business*, discusses the idiosyncrasies of English in tiresome detail, then corrects callers' grammar with priggish glee; a chat with a World War II denier; and an ATF expert on the growing nuclear capability of conceptual artists.
2 pm	**Talk of the Nation.** A recent report has identified a new, vaguely-defined, yet extremely serious problem facing America's children. A child psychologist, a Harvard sociologist, and a syndicated columnist tell how a concerned but mostly absent parent can cope with this issue.
3 pm	**Science Friday.** Live from Wood's Hole Oceanographic Institute: if a killer whale and a great white shark fought, who would win? How about two giant clams? Plus, the author of *Seahorse: Weirdo of the Deep.*
4 pm	**Fresh Air.** Host Terry Gross says "Fresh Air" with tremendous aspirative onomatopoeia, then interviews folksinger Buffy St. Marie; and the author of the new book, *Special Delivery: the Golden Age of the US Postal Service.*
5pm - 7 pm	**All Things Considered.** An extremely sedate round-up of today's catastrophes and mayhem, including Fran Leibowitz's death from writer's block. "The Loneliest Game": Profile of black players in NHL; an interview with the director of a new opera based on the life of Gorgeous George; "Sounds From the Archive": Mark Twain barking his shin and swearing. Plus: the 974th re-scoring of the ATC theme, this time for glockenspiel.
7 pm	**The World.** The bloody conflict in Kashmir: does it have anything to do with the sweaters? The Zep song?
8 pm	**Marketplace.** Today's financial news; plus, an exclusive investigation into whatever the hell "NASDAQ" stands for.
9 pm	**This American Life.** This week's theme: "VD." *Act I*: Monologues from America's next generation of *Harper's* writers, some of whom are afflicted with genital warts; *Act II*: David Sedaris reads a story about faking the clap at age eight; *Act III*: an unattended tape recorder is left on in the waiting room of a free clinic in San Diego; *Act IV*: Dan Savage unsympathetically discusses awful sexual diseases you never imagined possible.
10 pm	**On the Media.** (call-in show) Media figures discuss other media figures. Please do not call in (unless you are a media figure).
11 pm	**Jazz Set with Ed Bradley.** A celebration of Bix Biederbecke; "Would Dixieland Have Been Improved by Heroin?"; if Charlie Parker and Thelonious Monk fought, who would win? How about them versus two giant clams?
Mid.	**Newshour with Jim Lehrer Rebroadcast.** A positively soporific recapitulation of the day's disasters, in exhaustive detail; Shields and Gigot discuss the suspiciously fulsome hair of other Washington pundits; plus an essay by Richard Rosenblatt: "Is it Okay to Like Nixon Yet?"
1-5 am	**BBC News.** Hours of news with a patina of bitterness and snobbery, from today's faded empire to tomorrow's.

Mike & Jon • written 1998 • anthologized in *More Mirth of a Nation*, 2002

What is the FAFSA?

The **False Application for Federal Student Aid** is a spoof of the mind-numbing, yet strangely perky, form that millions of students use to mortgage their futures to pay for educational experiences of dubious utility. For many, particularly those in the liberal arts, the FAFSA is their last glimpse of debt-free existence for 20 years, or longer. Welcome to adulthood, ladies and gentlemen—start servicing that debt!

Hell, yes, we're bitter

We're loaded down, just like you are or will be. And why not? Four years of tuition at a private school can cost $130,000 or more. Public universities are cheaper, but there's no guarantee you'll get your money's worth there, either. (The University of Illinois, for example, now offers a class on Oprah Winfrey.) The worst part is, unlike in earlier generations, an undergraduate degree isn't enough; an M.B.A, M.D. or Ph.D. is now necessary to set yourself apart. Boy! we're getting depressed. Time to get to the jokes. Suffice to say…

Lasciate speranza, all ye who use this form to apply for student grants, work-study, and loans.

1. If you are filing a **2000 income tax return**, we recommend that you make it as believeable as possible. You don't need to file your tax return before submitting this form, but be warned that we won't believe that "Marijuana Depletion Allowance" nonsense. If you are going to college or, worse, grad school, simply because **you can't think of anything better to do**, fill out this form, then throw it in the garbage immediately. You'll thank us someday. You may also use this form to apply for **aid from other sources,** such as the Russian Mafia. You may be required to complete additional forms, or put up alarming items (relatives, kneecaps) as collateral. Check with your financial aid officer or strip club.

2. Your answers on this form will be misread electronically. Therefore:

- Fill in ovals completely.
- Please refrain from profanity.
- Crossing your sevens is affected.

Yes ● **No** ⊗ **No.** ✓ **No!** ○ **NO!!** ○

HOWTHEFUCKWILLIEVERPAYTHISBACK?

please remit $ 77,973 or face legal action

3. After you complete this form, make a copy for your records, to commemorate the exact date of your financial *Gotterdammerung*. Then send the original to: Enabling the Absurdly Inflated Cost of Higher Education, P.O. Box 4008, Mount Vernon, IL.

Step One: Fill out the form below.

1-4. Your full name

1. LAST NAME ____ **2.** FIRST NAME ____ **3.** MIDDLE INITIAL ____ **4.** STREET HANDLE ____

5-9. Where we can find and harass you (your apartment, parents' basement, friend's couch, the collapsing Bowery bakery where you're squatting)

6. YOUR STREET ☐☐☐☐☐☐☐☐☐☐☐☐☐☐ 7. CITY & COUNTRY ☐☐☐☐☐☐☐☐☐☐ 8. STATE ☐☐ 9. PHONE ☐☐☐☐☐☐☐☐☐☐

10. Describe your marital status.
- I am single, divorced, or widowed. ◯
- God! I would LOVE to be widowed. ◯
- I am married/remarried. ◯
- Same as above, but I "swing." ◯

11. What's your "sign"? ☐☐☐☐☐☐☐☐☐☐

12. Are you male? **Yes** ◯ **No** ◯

13. Sure? Look. **Yes** ◯ **No** ◯

14. If yes, can we register you with Selective Service? **Yes** ◯ **Yes** ◯

15. Okay, seriously: How many classes are you planning to cut? ☐☐ %

16. How many will you lose to cataclysmic drunkenness? ☐☐ %

17. And how many will you spend in, er, romantic interludes? ☐☐ %

If your total exceeds 100, find a cheaper way to have fun.

18. Do not leave this question blank. Have you ever smoked, ingested or otherwise consumed illegal drugs? If you have, answer "Yes," complete and submit this application, attaching a 1000 word essay on the funniest thing that ever happened to you when you were high. **Yes** ◯ **No** ◯

Step Two: Complete this worksheet.

19. Enter the total tuition you expect to pay. The amount increases daily; check www.tuitionticker .com for today's amount. $ ☐☐,☐☐☐
20. Multiply Line 19 by the current cost of Ramen Noodles: This is your total amount of scholarship. $ ☐,☐☐☐
21. Subtract Line 20 from Line 19. This is what you have to make in work study or loans. $ ☐☐,☐☐☐
22. Enter the current prime rate. Expressed decimally, this is your hourly wage. ☐.☐☐
23. Divide Line 21 by Line 22. These are the number of hours you must work, per year, to pay for school. ☐☐,☐☐☐
24. Screw that! Enter Line 21 here, then take a deep breath; this is how much in loans you will receive. $ ☐☐,☐☐☐

Step Three: Sign and date in blood or other legally-binding bodily fluid.

Mike
Village Voice
2001

Your Y2K Checklist

[In case you've forgotten, some experts believed that at midnight on December 31, 1999, most of the world's computers would stop functioning. We wrote a handy checklist to make sure you're prepared for all eventualities.]

Mike & Jon
More Mirth of a Nation
2002

Have you...

...written an apologetic letter to the Unabomber, acknowledging he was correct about the inevitable collapse of industrial society?
...trained yourself to disregard traffic lights?
...bought some playing cards?
...charged your taser?
...learned CPR, first aid, or—God forbid—effective home euthanasia?
...replaced "fluent in web design" on your resume with "can kill and dress wild game"?
...come up with descriptive-yet-devious code names for your friends and family?
...decided what animal your "Clan" will be named after?
...radically downgraded your expectations of personal hygiene, both for yourself and others?
...traded your new Boxster straight up for a diesel-burning, armor-plated school bus?
...begun to regret marrying for love rather than the ability to perform anesthesia-free appendectomies?
...concentrated on the bright side: that with the collapse of the magazine industry, soon there will be an entire generation of women without body image issues?
...asked your postman whether their slogan now reads "neither snow, nor rain, nor the inevitable collapse of industrial society as predicted by the Unabomber shall stay these couriers..."?
...discovered the phrase "panicked looting" doesn't have to have a negative connotation?
...started a meat-squirrel farm?
...reserved a gritty, resourceful babysitter?
...written down the names of all the states, along with the capitals of each, in case the government needs it?
...asked the rabbi whether or not grubs are kosher?
...propositioned those with whom you would most like to repopulate the world, if it comes to that? (Do not pick movie stars unless you live within walking distance of Hollywood.)
...come up with at least ten recipes in which pigeon can be substituted for chicken?
...taught yourself to use a litter box?
...created "collection trousers" to harvest your own methane?
...studied game theory to figure out to outwit someone at barter, every time?
...started, now that winter is here, to envy those with a high percentage of body fat?
...picked out a community member to ostracize and blame for all problems, from crop failures to plagues to children born with a caul?
...collected rocks with which to stone him/her to death?
...picked out a second community member to blame when problems continue, ideally a professor-type who makes irritating "appeals to reason"?
...collected more rocks with which to stone him/her to death?
...noticed that everyone seems to be keeping rocks near at hand?
...come to terms with the fact that, no matter what, you will continue to receive solicitations from the Quality Paperback Book Club?
...begun to truly understand the phrase, "the living will envy the dead"?
...identified the local children with the fewest useful skills and most nutritional value?
...learned not to be so smug about the Dark Ages?
...begun to find snide, half-clever jokes about Y2K much less funny? ☐

The Bible Code—SOLVED

To most, the claims of the new bestseller *The Bible Code*—that the major events of human history are encoded in the Hebrew Pentateuch supposedly dictated by God three millenia ago—must appear to be the ravings of a religious zealot, unscrupulous publicist, or unholy combination of the two. But as scholars who have devoted our lives to the text, we know the new book shows the merest tip of a truly titanic iceberg. We mourn the fact that its precious cargo of wisdom has been put on display in *The Bible Code* like so many dimestore geegaws. We also mourn that a misplaced sense of decency prevented us from rushing to press with our own book (tentatively titled *O.J., JonBenet, Tim McVeigh & the Bible*). As the Old Testament says, "Nice guys finish last" (Job 12:6). However, our wounds are salved by the fact that the only time the words "The Bible Code" appear in the actual Bible code, the phrase is intersected by "cataclysmically remaindered."

Mike & Jon
Seattle Weekly
1997

Our Method

There are 304,805 Hebrew characters in the first five books of the Old Testament, not counting crossouts. The characters were painstakingly entered into a Macintosh Quadra 610 by 50 temporaries using Microsoft Word 5.0; both the temps and the computers were chosen under strict rabbinical supervision.

Once the text was safely in Word, locating the prophecies was a simple matter of using the "Find" function (eg, "Find 'Bigfoot' and 'Apollo 11'.").

As a control, 304,805 contiguous characters from Dostoevesky's *Crime and Punishment* were translated into Hebrew, entered into the computer, then disregarded.

The Mysteries

1. What really happened at Roswell?

The word "Roswell" appears in the Code once, where it is crossed by "extraterrestrial" and the Hebrew year "5707"; a few lines below that, the phrase "weather balloon" can be located. Clearly, this means that in 1947, a weather balloon of alien origin crashed outside Corona, New Mexico. It was quickly confiscated by the Air Force, which discovered the temperature, humidity and barometric pressure on Alpha Centuri. Some say this is how we won the Cold War.

So, after 50 years of heated debate, the Air Force and legions of ufologists are BOTH right: it was a weather balloon, and it was from outer space. **Case closed!**

2. Who killed John F. Kennedy?

President Kennedy, in the words of the Code, "was shot by Lee Harvey Oswald, acting alone." However, so was his brother Robert. **Case closed!**

3. Did Hitler die at the end of World War II?

It depends on what you mean by "die."

The name "Adolf Hitler" appears verbatim in the text seven times. (The odds against this happening randomly have been calculated at roughly seventeen million to one.) By analyzing the words that surround and cross it, according to the Code, der Fuhrer was cloned in Brazil in 1947, using an eyelash smuggled out of his bunker during the last days of World War II.

However, the Code continues, the clone, named "Bruno Hitler," showed no charisma whatsoever. After failing eight consecutive times to win a spot on the Sao Paolo City Council, he was released from his contract in the early 1970's. He currently works as an actuary in Florida. For more information, contact: B. Hitler, Box 27, Boca Raton, FL 09124. **Case closed!**

4. What happened to Amelia Earhart?
The Bible Code reveals that famed aviatrix Amelia Earhart did not die somewhere in the South Pacific in 1937, when her twin-engine Electra ran out of fuel. Swimming to nearby Howland Island, she fashioned a sturdy raft out of coconut husks and bamboo. Riding her Kon-Tiki-like contraption on friendly currents to Mexico, Amelia joined a circus, and later, the Truman Administration. She now coaches field hockey at Stanford. **Case closed!**
5. Is Paul McCartney dead?
According to the Bible Code, Paul McCartney did in fact die in a car accident in 1966. He was replaced by the winner of a look-alike contest in Scotland named William Campbell. All of the clues on the Beatles' album covers and in their songs are 100% true. Oh, and the Code also says that guitarist Denny Laine wrote all of Wings' good songs, too. **Case closed!**
6. Just what was on the infamous "16 minute gap"?
Twenty-five years after the Watergate scandal, these 16 minutes of silence—blamed by Nixon on his secretary's mechanical incompetence—remain a mystery. Until the Bible Code, that is.

It turns out that the tapes contained not political secrets, but instead a torrid phone sex session between President Nixon and novelist/raconteur/gadfly Gore Vidal. Nearby the text contains the phrases "rosy Prexy bottom", "the judicious application of Vicks Vapo-rub" and "traditional Quaker wedding." Vidal has bragged for many years that he and the Chief Executive were engaged to be married in late 1974; until the Code, there existed no hard information proving this.

Vidal has intimated similar liasons with every President from Truman to Reagan, but on these matters the Code is mum. One suspects an overactive imagination. **Case closed!**
7. Does President Clinton have anything to fear from Paula Jones?
Emphatically so, according to the Bible Code. "President Bill Clinton"—or sometimes "President Chubs Pokorny" (?) — is found several times throughout the Book of Numbers. A close reading of the Bible Code reveals that the President does indeed have a distinguishing mark on his genitals: a small tattoo reading "I'm with stupid," with a tiny arrow pointing upwards. Whatever the implications for the Clinton Administration—and anyone but the staunchest supporter would agree that the Code does not augur well—the presence of the sleazy slogan in a work dictated by God over three millenia ago is impressive. **Case still open!**
9. Did the author of The Bible Code, *under orders from Simon & Schuster, kill Rabin himself, and attempt to start a nuclear armageddon?*
The Pentateuch ain't saying, but it'd be a great way to move some books, don't you think? **Case still open!** □

One agent was very interested in our doing a parody of <u>The Bible Code</u>. "I'm heading to the Hamptons for the weekend," he told us, "but if you guys can find a code in the 1040 by Monday, I think we've got something." Unfortunately, God neglected to hide a code in IRS Form 1040.

Double Diamond, Highest Difficulty

Mike & Jon • *The New Yorker* • May 2001

Across

1 This never happened
5 Schrödinger's dog
10 Half of zero
15 A stitch in _______ saves eight
19 Discredited alchemist
23 Book: The _______
25 Nonsense word
27 She was never President
28 Overhyped dot-com
30 Chevy Chase flop
32 Ugliest fruit
34 Woody Allen flick set in N.Y.C.
37 Lincoln: "I love _______"
40 Bald N.B.A.er
41 Obsolete computer language
46 Better not write this one in ink
47 Bee's remorse
48 Earhart's grave
55 Opposite of red
56 Not "gnu"
58 Famously foul-mouthed Canadian
59 Gandhi punched him

Down

2 Real captain of Pequod
3 Famous first words
4 Frost poem about "bumpin' uglies"
5 He died in Second World War
7 TV's crime-fighting slug
8 John _______
9 Common crossword mistake
12 Tarnished child star
13 Patron saint of zombies
14 Yoko (not "Ono")
15 Feed a cold, starve a fever, _______ hookworm
16 It's immune to gravity
17 The aunt of invention
18 Harpo quote
24 Sixteenth sense
26 Slept with Warren Beatty
32 "Sayonara" in dolphin
34 Sec. of State, 1836-42, dog
35 2 + 2 DOESN'T equal…
36 Military acronym
41 What happens after you die
43 "The Next Beatles"
51 Jesus Christ's daughter
56 Long-running anarchist sitcom □

The Knowledge Tree

Course Catalog • Summer 1999 • "America's Largest Source of Adult Education Tinged with An Existential Sadness Since 1969"sm

Mike & Jon
More Mirth of a Nation
July 1999

Self-Esteem Secrets of the Aztecs

Ever wondered how they built all those step-pyramids? Central America's loaded with 'em, and every single one is proof that when you feel great about yourself, anything's possible! People from Charles Manson to legal eagle Alan Dershowitz have used the ancient wisdom of the Aztecs to increase their self-esteem and reach their goals. Now, thanks to archaeotherapist and healer **Misha Witherspoon** (*Harnessing Your Hummingbird; You're OK, I'm Quetzalcoatl*), you can too! In one fascinating/terrifying evening, Misha will show you how to outsmart the fearsome jaguars of negativity and sacrifice your doubts on the bloody altar of SUCCESS! **Course 919 • Midtown • Members: $39/Non-members: $49**

Ride the "Gray Wave" to Prosperity!

How to Bilk the Elderly

As America's population ages, more and more money is concentrated in the hands of one group: senior citizens. Starved for companionship or merely interaction, often disoriented by medication, the elderly are the perfect target for con men, sharpies, grifters or anybody who needs a little extra cash. **Dr. Dev Bhat**, author of *If They've Got a Will, There's a Way*, has been #1 on the AARP's Most Wanted List since 1982. He'll show you: how a sympathetic smile can be worth million$...how to use nostalgia to build trust...the placebo gambit...how to cut faraway relatives out of the picture...and much more! **Course 401 • Midtown • Members: $39/Non-members: $49**

An Evening With Donovan's Brother

What it's like to be related to a rock star? Find out as **Steven Leitch**, Donovan's brother since 1949, joins us for an evening of fun, music and memories! Steven spent most of "The 60s" at his brother's side, living the high-powered life of a roadie/gofer. He'll give you the inside scoop on how it felt to watch his idiot baby brother rocket to the Top of the Pops, including: fielding phone calls from Mick, Paul, Janis and Loudon; where to find a sitar string in Leicester at 2 AM; the not-so-hidden meanings in "Green Tambourine"; lickety-split home remedies for crab lice; and so much more! **Course 433 • Midtown Members: $39/Non-members: $49**

Writing Children's Erotica

Combine Two Hot Genres for a Sure-fire Bestseller!

Twelve months ago, no one in publishing would've predicted that erotica for children would grow into a $2 billion-a-year industry! And they were right, it hasn't. But maybe it will someday, so here's your chance to get in on the ground floor. The hitch, of course, is that even the field's experts aren't sure what children's erotica is or could possibly be. Nevertheless, certified non-perv **Wilma Freedrick** will give it her best shot, as she tries to teach you to, in her words, "describe colors to a blind person." **Course 981 • Midtown Members: $69/Non-members: $79**

Attacked By the Light

An Empowering, Dispiriting Event with BARRY LANSKY

In 1993, **Barry Lansky** was in a car wreck and pronounced dead at the scene. His soul left his body and traveled through a tunnel. At the end he was greeted by a being of light, which emanated love, joy and compassion…and then beat him. Savagely.

Since then, Lansky has been telling people what Heaven is *really* like. In this incredibly depressing class you'll learn: why, if they ask, always choose "return to Earth!"…three moves men can use when God tries to kick them in the 'nads…and how to avoid real estate scams fronted by your dead relatives. If you're planning on dying, don't miss it! **Course 673 • Midtown • Members: $39/Non-members: $49**

Copyrighting Things That Have Already Been Invented

How many times have you thought, "Man, I bet whoever copyrighted kissing has a lot of money." Well, you're right, he does—it's Steve Metz, of La Jolla, California. Did people kiss before Steve filed for copyright? Sure. But now he can sue anyone—even the President—who kisses anything without paying him $.0005 per smooch.

In one avaricious evening, lecturer David Golden (himself the owner of the copyright on "lecturing") will show you how a typo in the 1978 Copyright Law can make you rich literally overnight. But only if you're quicker than the next guy, so register today! (All words and ideas in this course description ©1999 David Golden. Your thoughts as you read that are also ©1999 D.G.) **Course 414 • Midtown • Members: $39/Non-members: $69**

We're sorry, but as of press time the following classes were filled. Be sure to check back next semester! Comb-Over Master Class • Be An Ugliness Model • Past-Life Psychoanalyst • Beat the Tarot • Reduce Your Vocabulary Today • How to Seduce Animals • You CAN Marry Poor • Kill With Feng Shui • Punishing Your Inner Child • Worthless Computer Skills • Breaking Out of TV • Braille for the Sighted • Travel the World by Mail • Learn Swing-Fu... ☐

Sometimes, if we really liked a piece, we'd lay out a few pages to see if it might work as a book. Editors always liked these; some even asked if they could keep 'em to show to friends. Then they told us "no thanks."

44 • The Knowledge Tree Course Catalog * Summer 1999

Co-Sponsored by the NY Association for Quiet Desperation (www.ny-desperation.com)

Self-Esteem Secrets of the Aztecs

(Headshot)

Ever wondered how they built all those step-pyramids? Central America's loaded with them; proof that when you feel great about yourself, anything's possible! People from Charles Manson to legal eagle Alan Dershowitz have used the ancient wisdom of the Aztecs to increase their self-esteem and reach their goals. Now, thanks to archaeotherapist and healer **Misha Witherspoon** (*Harnessing Your Hummingbird, You're OK, I'm Quetzaalcoatl*), you can too! In one fascinating/terrifying evening, Misha will show you how to outsmart the fearsome jaguars of negativity and sacrifice your doubts on the bloody altar of SUCCESS!

Course 919 Midtown
Members: $39/Non-members: $49

Ride the "Gray Wave" to Prosperity

How to Bilk the Elderly

Highly Illegal!

As America's population ages, more and more money is concentrated in the hands of one group: senior citizens. Starved for companionship or merely interaction, often disoriented from medication, the elderly are the perfect target for con men, sharpies, grifters or anybody who needs a little extra cash.

Dr. Dev Bhat, author of *If They've Got a Will, There's a Way*, has been #1 on the AARP's Most Wanted List since 1982. He'll show you: • how a sympathetic smile can be worth million$ • using nostalgia to build trust • the placebo gambit • replacing faraway relatives • and much more!

Course 401 Midtown
Members: $39/Non-members: $49

Attacked By the Light

An Empowering, Dispiriting Event with **BARRY LANSKY**

In 1993, Barry Lansky was in a car wreck and pronounced dead at the scene. His soul left his body and traveled through a tunnel. At the end he was greeted by a being of light, which emanated love, joy and compassion… and then beat him. Savagely.

Since then, Lansky has been telling people what Heaven is *really* like. In this incredibly depressing class you'll learn: • why, if they ask, always choose "return to earth" • three moves men can use when God tries to kick them in the 'nads • and how to avoid real estate scams fronted by your dead relatives. If you're planning on dying, don't miss it!

Course 673 Midtown
Members: $39/Non-members: $49

Writing Children's Erotica

Dirty!

Combine Two Hot Genres for a Sure-fire Bestseller!

Twelve months ago, no one in publishing would've predicted that erotica for children would grow into a $2 billion-a-year industry! And they were right, it hasn't. But maybe it will someday, so here's your chance to get in on the ground floor. The hitch, of course, is that even the field's experts aren't sure what children's erotica is or could possibly be. Nevertheless, certified non-perv **Wilma Freedrick** will give it her best shot, as she tries to teach you to, in her words, "describe colors to a blind person."

Course 981 Midtown
Members: $69/Non-members: $79

Copyrighting Things That Have Already Been Invented

How many times have you thought, "Man, I bet whoever copyrighted kissing has a lot of money." Well, you're right, he does—it's Steve Metz, of La Jolla, California. Did people kiss before Steve filed for copyright? Sure. But now he can sue anyone—even the President—who kisses anything without paying him $.0005 per smooch.

In one avaricious evening, lecturer **David Golden** (himself the owner of the copyright on "lecturing") will show you how a typo in the 1978 Copyright Law can make you rich literally overnight. But only if you're quicker than the next guy, so register today! (*All words and ideas in this course description ©1999 David Golden. Your thoughts as you read that are also ©1999 D.G.*)

Course 414 Midtown
Members: $29/Non-members: $69

Too Late!

We're sorry, but as of press timethe following classes were filled. Be sure to check back next semester!

Comb-Over Master Class
Be An Ugliness Model
Past-Life Psychoanalyst
Beat the Tarot
Reduce Your Vocabulary Today
How to Seduce Animals
You CAN Marry Poor
Kill With Feng Shui
Punishing Your Inner Child
Worthless Computer Skills
Breaking Out of TV
Braille for the Sighted
Travel the World by Mail
Learn Swing-Fu

An Evening With Donovan's Brother

What it's like to be related to a rock star? Find out as **Steven Leitch**, Donovan's brother since 1949, joins us for an evening of fun, music and memories! Steven spent most of "The 60s" at his brother's side, living the high-powered life of a roadie/gofer. He'll give you the inside scoop on how it felt to watch his idiot baby brother rocket to the Top of the Pops, including: • fielding phone calls from Mick, Paul, Janis and Loudon • where to find a sitar string in Leicester at 2 AM • the not-so-hidden meanings in "Green Tambourine" • lickety-split home remedies for crab lice •and much more!

Course 433 Midtown
Members: $39/Non-members: $49

* Since 1969, America's Largest Source of Adult Education Tinged with An Existential Sadness"℠

Candidates From The Shadows

Mike & Jon
August 2002

Fellow Citizens:
We come before you today to announce our joint candidacy for the presidency of the United States.

We know that the media, with their endless lust for "scandal," will dig this up eventually, so let us be the first to admit that we are (1) under 35 and thus Constitutionally ineligible; (2) totally unqualified; and (3) not sure which party we belong to.

Let's address these objections in turn.

First: it is true that we are both under 35, but our combined age lifts us over the Constitution's ageist bar with decades to spare. In our youth-oriented era, it is well-past time to smash the superstition that only one adult can be President at once. Two heads, even ours, are better than one. And who is to say that the U.S. wouldn't do better with a future Co-Presidency of three internet-savvy twelve year-olds -- or even five extremely bright seven year-olds? Before you answer, remember that the President was once Gerald Ford.

Second, like George W. Bush, we have no idea who the Prime Minister of India is. We also cannot locate India on a map. And every time we leave the house, we have to write our address on the inside of our arms. But there's something else we don't know--are you listening, political elites?--we don't know when we're licked!

Third, it's true that we're not sure whether we're Democrats or Republicans. But neither does Bill Gates, whose company has given $1 million to both parties' conventions. We plan to follow Microsoft's lead and have both parties nominate us, eliminating the time-consuming competition that has clogged American politics for so long.

Since both our parties agree on just about everything, we hadn't planned on coming up with any distinct positions; we were just going to show up at the conventions and "look Co-Presidential." In a normal election year, that would be fine. Unfortunately, we're told that Common Cause, Call to Renewal, United for a Fair Economy, the Lindesmith Center, Arianna Huffington, and others are convening "shadow conventions" in both Philadelphia and Los Angeles to focus on three key issues: Poverty and the Wealth Gap, Campaign Finance Reform, and the Failed Drug War. Frankly, we resent them stirring things up, but after a crowded five minutes, we came up with simple, effective solutions in all three areas.

Poverty and the Wealth Gap

In 1973, the top 1% of America's households owned 23% of the nation's wealth; today, their share has almost doubled to 44%. This is a great start, but we have a long way to go. We think that nurses, teachers and firemen have gotten a free ride for too long, while CEOs and bond traders scrape by with only three Gulfstream Vs. America, we must do better.

Of course, a few people may complain when a squad of government roughnecks repossess their house so it can be handed over to Warren Buffet. Some may even ask what Mr. Buffet will do with several million homes. The answer is: whatever he wants to. And friends, that's what Freedom is about.

Campaign Finance Reform

During the 1988 campaigns, the Democrats and Republicans raised about $45 million in unregulated "soft money," but the 2000 edition is expected to bring in ten times as much

-- up to half a billion dollars. Clearly, this process is totally out of control. We must stop counting every penny! We're all Americans here, why the formality? If paper bags filled with cash were good enough for Spiro Agnew, it's good enough for us. If elected, we will institute a simple, straightforward system of flagrant bribery.

The Failed War on Drugs

It's estimated that by the end of 2001, America will have a prison population of two million, four times higher than in 1980 and greater than that of China and Russia. Still, this is no time to rest on our laurels -- now that we've captured the lead, we should take this opportunity to "run up the score" and put the game out of reach. Remember, two million sounds impressive, but that means that 258 million of us remain unincarcerated.

Finally, most of our burgeoning prison population is attributable to the War on Drugs, but we have yet to take the logical step of shooting at the drugs themselves. We have a huge defense budget -- why not spend some of that money training the Marines for amphibious assaults on big piles of marijuana?

Thanks for your time -- and we'll see you in the voting booth November 7th! God bless you, and when we're elected, may god bless America! □

We CAN Be Bought!

With the orgy of GOP fundraising going on this week, we here at The Shadow Convention are feeling rather left out. Why, why, WHY is no one trying to bribe us? Isn't our influence just as good as the next guy's? And we have a range of prices to fit any influence-peddling budget.

Friends, forget voting—only by greasing the Shadow Convention can you participate in the almost-sacred process of electing our next President. Help us take our rightful place at the trough—donate today!

Item	Price[1]
Complete betrayal of our principles	
In public	$1000.00
In private	$350.00
A high-level post in hypothetical Franken Administration	$250.00
"Shadow Judgeship" for yourself, your spouse, your child, or pet	$200.00
Permit to fill the Annenberg Center with toxic waste of your choice	$150.00
Flyfishing with Chuck D	$100.00
A Happy Meal at the McDonald's on 40th and Walnut with Lewis Lapham	$75.00
72 holes of golf with your Shadow caddy, "Granny D"	$50.00
Hot-oil message/explication of American poverty by Jonathan Kozol	$25.00
Bamboo backscratcher signed by Arianna Huffington	$7.50
"Stamp Out Poverty" novelty insoles	$3.50

(1) slightly higher in Canada.

In 2000, we were invited to Arianna Huffington's "Shadow Conventions," a gathering of the progressive/liberal tribes at the sites of the Democratic and Republican conventions. Our job was to provide satire to order, on the issues of corporate greed, party corruption, and the failed War on Drugs. This was a little handout we created on the back of a dollar bill.

The Contract

Mike & Jon
July 2002

THIS AGREEMENT is entered into this ___ day of July, 1997, by and between Harold Cohagan of Working Lunch Communications, Inc., a corporation organized under the laws of the state of—guess where—New York, and having a place of business in—guess where—midtown Manhattan ("the Agent"), and Joshua Glottal, a young-ish writer who still hasn't gotten over a painful adolescence, having a dingy residence in Park Slope, Brooklyn ("the Author").

WHEREAS the Author has always intended to produce numerous fat novels explaining precisely where America went wrong; and

WHEREAS slipping "my agent says..." into casual conversation would make the Author feel better about having to temp; and

WHEREAS it's probably too late for the Author to go back to school and get a job in computer animation; and

WHEREAS the Agent majored in English and once thought of writing but realized that going out to lunch on your expense account is more fun than sitting in a room by yourself deciding whether to use "irritable" or "petulant"; and

WHEREAS the Agent is rapidly realizing it would be even more fun to represent movie stars instead of people who, the Agent surmises, cut their own hair, but nevertheless;

NOW, THEREFORE, in consideration of the foregoing premises and the mutual covenants set forth below and other valuable considerations, the parties agree as follows:

I. Services. The Author appoints the Agent to act as his representative in negotiating agreements for the publication of his work, whether conventionally, electronically, or, in the future, via a yarmulke-like device that pumps images directly into the user's visual cortex.

A. The Author agrees to be genuinely thrilled when the Agent manages to sell his first book, *Cain's Children,* to a minuscule, cash-starved press in Vermont, for an advance barely sufficient to buy a new pair of glasses.

B. The Agent agrees to let slip that his girlfriend from college is now a booker for "Oprah" and, by not saying anything more, allow the author's fantasies to burgeon until he has to lie down in the dark with a cold washcloth on his head.

C. The Agent agrees to field up to ten (10) phone calls per day listening to the Author's ever more outlandish theories on why the book isn't selling, followed by the mantra-like repetition of a review in *Ephemera* saying the Author's work "out Angelous-Angelou," whatever the hell that means.

D. The Agent agrees to pretend that it's his mother calling, instead of his other client with the lucrative *Spinebenders* series of horror novels for preteens with its many profitable marketing spin-offs including *Spinebenders* gum which makes your spit look like blood.

E. When his career sputters, the Author agrees to bombard the agent with phone calls asking why Martin Amis is getting the advances that he, the Author, should be getting, and maybe he should get Martin Amis' agent, *goddammit.*

F. After the Author gets divorced in middle age, he agrees to hang around the Agent's office attempting to pick up the female interns; further, the Agent agrees not to represent the Author's ex-spouse in any embarrassing tell-all memoir.

G. The Author authorizes the Agent to anonymously initiate a fatwah against the Author, if in the Agent's judgment this will generate sales or a piece in *The New York Times Sunday Magazine.* Any fatwah must be pre-approved by the Author.

H. If, to everyone's surprise, the Author actually gets killed, the Agent agrees to compare the Author to both Jonathan Swift and Ken Saro-Wiwa at the funeral, and afterwards make tasteless jokes about how he, the Agent, is now 15% dead. (see Commissions, Section II.A, below)

II. Compensation

A. Commission As compensation for the above-referenced services, the Agent shall receive a commission in the amount of fifteen percent (15%) of all royalties due the Author. The Author shall weekly calculate how much this 15%, *which is rightfully his,* would yield if invested in a good mutual fund. The Author will also hang around with other disgruntled Authors and hatch half-baked schemes in which the Authors will represent each other.

B. Other Payments The Author will be increasingly irritated if the Agent can't drum up some movie interest, particularly in the case of his last pre-fatwah book, *Double Kill Action,* featuring protagonist Jack Crane, "a dead-ringer for Tom Cruise, Harrison Ford, and/or Wesley Snipes."

C. No Return of Commissions If the Author receives an advance based on three chapters of a novel about a popular President who's a serial killer, and then turns in a 1,400 page fictionalization of his childhood, the Agent gets to keep *his* 15%.

D. Expenses The Author will reimburse the Agent for any reasonable expenses, including the installation of caller ID, an unlisted phone number, an abrupt change of the Agent's place of business, or any other steps necessary to evade the Author as their relationship deteriorates.

III. Termination This contract may be terminated by either party or when the publishing industry finally collapses, whichever comes first.

IN WITNESS WHEREOF, the parties have signed this Agreement as of the date set forth above.

______________________ ______________________

Joshua Glottal Harold Cohagan ☐

The Homer Hall of Fame

Mike & Jon
August 1998

Any student of the game will tell you that hitting a baseball is one of the hardest things in sports. And whacking that ball a quarter-mile against major-league pitching demands almost superhuman skill. So, as Mark McGwire and Sammy Sosa swat and swipe ever-closer to Roger Maris' record for home runs in a season, fans everywhere wonder: how do they do it? Most say it's pure natural ability (plus a dash of androstenedione). Others point to a "live ball" or diluted pitching talent. And Pierre Salinger claims he found a document on the Internet proving that "Moon Men" have lessened the earth's gravitational pull. We've looked into the issue, and as the list below shows, each slugger carves a unique path into homer history.

61--Roger Maris (1961)
Even though it has now stood for longer than Ruth's fabled 60, Maris's record has always been saddled with an asterisk. Not only did his sixty-one homers come during a longer season, purists also object to the league-wide gentlemen's agreement to pitch underhand to Maris after July 15.

60--Babe Ruth (1927)
According to Ring Lardner, Yankee manager Miller Huggins unlocked Ruth's potential by telling him there was a six-pack, ten hot dogs, and a hooker hidden between third and home. The Babe fell for this not just once, but *714 times* during his career, which should tell you something.

59--Babe Ruth (1921)
The highest total during the "square ball era," which lasted from 1890 until advances in nutrition made Americans smarter. Even more impressive, Ruth eschewed a bat until 1923, preferring to swing the palm of his hand. (His callous, weighing nearly eight pounds, is now displayed at the Army's Walter Reed Medical Museum.)

58--Mark McGwire (1997)
McGwire brings three things with him to the plate: (1) tremendous strength, (2) a natural uppercut swing, and (3) a very distracting chow dog. The chow's piercing yips often so discombobulate pitchers, that they serve up hanging curves which McGwire laughingly belts into the bleachers.

58--Jimmie Foxx (1932)
While Ruth used to "call" the location of his homers before hitting them, only "Double X" did this for grounders and foul balls as well. Games were sometimes delayed as Foxx -- called the politest man ever to play the game -- trotted out to inform infielders exactly where to stand to intercept the ball.

58--Hank Greenberg (1938)
The only Jewish slugger on our list, Greenberg harnessed the terrifying power of the Kabbalah to make his ball fly farther. "Hammerin' Hank" hired 30 rabbis to sit in the Detroit outfield and "draw the ball to them, as with a golden cord." His career took a nose-dive the next year, after the League passed a rule prohibiting the use of supernatural forces.

56--Ken Griffey, Jr. (1997)
Not only does Junior have a chance to beat Maris' mark every season he plays, he seems certain to challenge Hank Aaron's 755 career dingers. Disgruntled opponents accuse him of using hypnosis on pitchers. They also accuse him of hypnotizing the League officials investigating their claim. Now, a rumor is circulating that Griffey can somehow hypnotize the ball. "This conspiracy reaches to the highest levels of the American government," says Pierre Salinger.

56--Hack Wilson (1930)
Hack Wilson became so celebrated during his run at Ruth's record that a popular, phlegm-producing cough was named after him. Prior to that, it had been called the "Babe."

55--Mike Gerber and Jon Schwarz (1990)
During their brief, remarkable career, this pair used to stand on either side of the plate and swing simultaneously. They tore the cover off the ball, in the few cases they didn't break each other's ribs. The mark was thrown out after videotape showed that the duo wasn't playing for either team. "The streetclothes tipped us off," said AL President Gene Budig. □

The Lust Generation

Mike & Jon
September 1998

"In August, Scribner's announced it will release 'True At First Light,' Ernest Hemingway's last unpublished novel, in time for the author's centenary next July 21. Edited by his son Patrick, the 200,000-word manuscript is a fictionalized account of an African safari Hemingway took in 1953.[...]Along with ruminations on Paris, religion, Ezra Pound and baseball, the book reveals that while in Kenya Hemingway married a pair of Wakamba tribeswomen, an 18 year old named "Debba" and her 17-year-old sister. Hemingway's wife Mary consented to the bizarre union, provided that Debba 'first have a much-needed bath.'"
—*news item*

As shocking as Hemingway's two-toned three-way would have been to Fifties America, society-defying love was the norm among the artists and writers who made up his "Lost Generation." Edmund Wilson quipped that "they wouldn't have been so 'Lost' if they'd spent more than three nights in the same bed." For example, Edna St. Vincent Millay scoured census records in her quest to sample every male below Fourteenth Street; her nickname, "The Biological Clock," stemmed from her taking and spurning 24 lovers in one remarkable, parts-chafing day. Friends always maintained that this was a frantic search for true love, and claimed she never got over gentlemen Nine through Thirteen. But not everyone was so generous. "What do Edna and marching soldiers have in common?" asked Dorothy Parker. "Tramp, tramp, tramp."

Simultaneously, Millay herself was being pursued by Round Tabler Edna Ferber—apparently a woman of surpassing narcissism—who fell for Millay "because of that exquisite first name of hers." Ferber managed to lure the poetess down to City Hall to get hitched, but during the ceremony the lights went out and Ferber somehow ended up married to herself. The union soon collapsed in a bitter divorce, and Ferber often complained she was being ruined by alimony payments. Still, she was not yet soured on matrimony: during the Twenties she married no fewer than thirty-four women, some without their knowledge. However, after reading that she had herself been married in absentia by a group of schoolteachers from Brooklyn, Ferber declared, "The hell with it," and began a less complicated new life in Hollywood.

Literary bellwether F. Scott Fitzgerald took even greater pleasure in flouting convention, and for six months in 1919 lived in sin with four Austrian girls and a banded krait. The quintet never married—the lethal snake bit the women in a jealous rage, then moved in with Hart Crane—but Fitzgerald's biographer Jerome Tebbler quotes him as calling it "my first adult relationship."

But Fitzgerald was trumped almost daily as romantic experimentation turned into blind frenzy. Dorothy Rothschild became "Mrs. Parker" after suffering through a brief, stormy marriage to a Parker brand tricycle. Left at the altar by a kazoo, she twice married Alan Campbell, a writer/actor/paperweight, and found him very useful on her desk. Later, in an ill-fated effort to free Sacco and Vanzetti, radical Max Eastman wed a copy of *Das Kapital* on the steps of the Lincoln Memorial. In a fitting climax to the craze, John Dos Passos married the concept of Anarcho-Syndicalism in June 1929. He later confided to friends that during this period of his life he was "very confused."

After the Crash, matrimony returned to normal—almost. Not influenced artistically by Fitzgerald and his set, William Faulkner was impressed by their unorthodox domestic arrangements, although he felt there had to be some "middle way" that defied convention without engaging in either promiscuity or liaisons with inanimate objects. This belief led Faulkner, in late 1932, to become the first man south of the Mason-Dixon line to cohabitate with a plant. Faulkner lived with the plant, a rubber tree he called "Jenny," for seven months until she left him for a ficus. When the ficus died less than a year later, many suspected Faulkner, but he strenuously denied the rumors, blaming a fungus called "bunt, or stinking smut." The author never got over Jenny's betrayal; the first draft of his Nobel acceptance speech read "I believe that Man shall not just endure, he shall triumph...over that damn ficus. And bunt."

Given this historical background, Hemingway's brief jaunt into interracial polygamy is hardly worth mentioning. Still, it may be enough to make "True at First Light" unwelcome in high schools throughout the South, which puts it in some fine company. It seems appropriate that the author of the oft-banned "Great Gatsby" has the final word. "The rich are different from you and I," Scott Fitzgerald once remarked wearily. "For one, they're not in love with a frickin' poisonous snake." □

Jon
Weekend Update
1998

An Indiana convict who actually asked to be executed for the murder of another inmate was killed by lethal injection last week. His final words? "That's the LAST time I try reverse psychology."

Mike
Weekend Update
1998

Police in California are looking for the killer – or killers – of a dozen sea lions, some of which were decapitated. Reached for comment, O.J. Simpson said, "I really resent whatever joke you're about to make."

Jon
Weekend Update
1998

Star Utah Jazz forward Karl Malone says he has gotten a permit to carry a concealed weapon. He's also changing his nickname from "The Mailman" to "The Disgruntled Mailman."

Jon
Weekend Update
1998

Last Sunday, Monica Lewinsky toured the birthplace of American democracy, Philadelphia's Independence Hall. In a statement to the press, she called the many exhibits about the Founding Fathers "mouth-watering."

The Worst Football Team of the 20th Century

Mike & Jon
Seattle Weekly
September 1999

SCOUT'S NOTES (OFFENSE)

QB – James Joyce

Jim "The Passin' Polymath" Joyce is nearly blind and insists on calling the signals using a patois of foreign languages, inside jokes, and cultural ephemera. His book, "Portrait of the Artist as a Rookie" (Routledge), infuriated some teammates after it questioned their skill, desire, and academic credentials.

Fullback – Shirley Temple

Nimble, but the 63 pound Temple is no blocking back. It's awful to watch her get brutalized, play after play, until she's nothing but a mass of contusions and shredded taffeta. On a famous end-around against the Bears, she started belting out "The Good Ship Lollipop" but only got to "Shi--" before being knocked unconscious.

Halfback – Gertrude Stein

"Sarge" Stein runs the forty in three minutes and grunts to herself constantly. Teammates suspect that she's making up different rules and playing by them; on the plus side, doesn't need separate locker facilities.

Wide Receiver – Charles Manson

Disruptive and weaselly, Chuck Manson delights in convincing weak-minded teammates that (1) he's Jesus Christ and (2) America started the Second World War. At his most effective when left in the locker room -- if he's not visible, opponents start to worry he's at their homes, welding their wives and children into another murderous commune.

Wide Receiver – Rupert Murdoch

66 year old media titan Murdoch always starts, because he owns the team. Some feel he has degraded the game with the introduction of topless cheerleaders. Others, by his mere presence on the field.

Left Tackle – Ferdinand Marcos

"The puniest strongman ever squeezed from the loins of Totalitarianism" (Inside Sport), Marcos benches thirty-seven pounds, and that's with an updraft. Refuses to play if Imelda isn't allowed to sing "The Star Spangled Banner."

Left Guard – Seka

Although quite well-liked by teammates, this early eighties porn starlet is the weakest link in any chain. Still, she tells fascinating stories about John Holmes, and has found hitherto undreamed-of uses for mouthguards and athletic tape. "A catastrophe in cleats," said Frank Deford. "But somehow, I don't care."

Center – Antonio Gramsci

"Red Dog" Gramsci, a 4'10" hunchback from Sardinia A&M, is widely considered the worst draft pick in NFL history. He's the unhappy fruit of George Halas' brief, impassioned infatuation with Italian Communist theory.

Right Guard – Quentin Crisp
With pass rushers faster than ever, "Q-Tip" Crisp is woefully overmatched. Say scouts, "For one quarter, it's 'Hey, he wrote *The Naked Civil Servant!* I totally dug that!' Then they get over it and take Q-Tip to school."

Right Tackle – Milton Friedman
Two things Milt Friedman has to answer for: Thatcherism, and allowing 4.5 sacks/game. "The doctrines of monetarism are useless against a good swim-move," says one coach.

Tight End – Kurt Cobain
Cobain's addiction to heroin makes him one of the most sluggish receivers ever to play the game. Trapped in a miasma of depression, he will drop anything thrown his way, and then write a power-pop anthem about how he secretly likes losing.

SCOUT'S NOTES (DEFENSE)
Cornerback -- Yukio Mishima
Sensitive about his 5'2" height, Mishima is the only player ever to wear platform cleats. If he gets beaten deep, the trainer must keep an eye on him, or he'll try to commit ritual suicide. Also, his rabid ideology is a big turnoff for fans who are not Japanese militarists.

Cornerback – William Burroughs
Burroughs carries a gun, and has knocked off three teammates "by accident." Claims to love football, although he refers to it "the Green Shit funneled through America's Patriotic Guts."

Free Safety – Gregorin Rasputin
"The Mad Monk" emits a powerful odor, and is mostly interested in seducing the cheerleaders (topless or not). He and Burroughs have staring contests that creep everybody out.

Strong Safety – Andy Rooney
One of the most unreliable players ever to wear a helmet, Rooney never shows up until the last few minutes of the game, at which point he delivers a curmudgeonly soliloquy about why he doesn't like ATMs.

Linebacker – Helen Keller
More proof that football and socialism don't mix, Hellen "Wheels" Keller is an inspiring story everywhere but on the gridiron. By the time her super-sensitive fingers meet the ballcarrier, he's by her and in the clear. Heartbreaking.

Middle Linebacker – Joseph Goebbels
Joe Goebbels is one of History's – and Football's – greatest monsters. Pumps out propaganda contending that the other team controls the world financial system. Whenever his side is losing, he exhorts them to fight harder, then slips away to swallow cyanide.

Outside Linebacker – Ruth Westheimer
Lusty, grandma-oid charm can't help Westheimer. "Imagine your Nana being pancaked by a 310-pound pulling guard," says a wincing GM. "It ain't pretty."

Defensive End – Jean-Paul Sartre
"Jack-P" gives minus-110% every play. Could compete, if he thought it mattered.

"Doesn't," says his new book.

Defensive Tackle – Andy Warhol
"A-Bomb" abhors human contact, a crippling disability in the trenches. His verite documentary of the '65 season, "Meat," is somehow 14 hours longer than the season itself. For serious football fans only. Actually, not even for them.

Defensive Tackle – Little Richard
If "Campiness" were a stat, Little Richard would be an All-Pro, but it's not. He lines up 20-30 yards away from the offense, then sprints in the opposite direction, loudly singing about Taco Bell. No one has caught him yet.

Defensive End – The Cast of "Friends"
These six lovable, neurotic, interchangeable urbanites are viciously pounded into the turf every game, to the delight of all.

Punter - William Howard Taft
"Bloated Bill"'s almost-unimaginable girth makes proper leg extension impossible. Longest kick: 17 inches, counting the ricochet off his paunch.

Kicker - Henri Toulouse-Lautrec
Lautrec combines an exquisite sensitivity and lack of size to be a uniquely useless player. "Hey, Lincoln wants his hat back." Claims physical exertion makes him gag.

COACH – Wilhelm Reich
Coach Reich is extremely popular among the players for his messianic faith in the power of the orgasm; this hasn't stopped him from being fired 26 times. Is quite a sight sitting on the sidelines in his orgone box. Vince Lombardi's nickname for Reich: "Easy Come, Easy Go." ☐

Over a hundred Muslims pilgrims died in a stampede in Mecca this week as they were performing a ritual known as "stoning the devil." Unfortunately, the Devil was performing a ritual known as "crushing the pilgrims."

Mike
Weekend Update
1998

This week Palestinian official announced that a new airport on the Gaza Strip will be named after Yasir Arafat. That's kind of like putting the Unabomber on a postage stamp.

Jon
Weekend Update
1998

A new drug, triptorelin, has been found to lessen the urges of pedophiles. "After only three doses, subjects no longer had any urge to listen to Hanson."

Mike
Weekend Update
1998

In an interview with Entertainment Tonight this week, Burt Reynolds announced that he is engaged to be married. Meanwhile, his toupee announced its engagement to a small cat.

Jon
Weekend Update
1998

A Vast Left-Wing Conspiracy

"Information has exposed Monica Lewinsky as a spy assigned by the former Soviet Union!"—Guandong Writer, China

"Monica Lewinsky is a young Jewish girl that Mossad hired [in] a plot fabricated by worldwide Zionism"—Al-Khaleej, United Arab Emirates

Mike & Jon
September 1998

And, finally:
"Scandal's Legacy: A Blush of Open Sex Talk"—*Washington Post*, February 12, 1999

Daddy—
I will never be able to thank you for all you've done during this horrible ordeal. From the moment the story broke, to my last testimony, I couldn't have survived without your love and support. I know I'm the luckiest daughter in the—

But no. As I peer through the porthole of this secret subterranean monorail, I know that the charade must end. You have loved me, "Dad," and though I will never see you again, I owe you one final gift: the truth. Prepare to encounter the most secret, far-reaching conspiracy in the history of Humanity!

The person you have known as "Monica" is a fraud, a fake, a lie. My name is Frank Hamblen; I am 53 years old, have sparse blond hair and a natural height of 6'4". Following extensive plastic surgery and training, I was switched with your newborn daughter 25 years ago. My top secret mission was to (1) cause the GOP to cripple itself well into the next century, and (2) make Americans more comfortable discussing oral sex.

On whose behalf did I act? The Mossad? After a fashion. And the KGB. And the CIA, the NSA, and WGBH Boston. For these organizations—along with many, many others worldwide—are tentacles of the most powerful, most secretive, most liberal cabal on Earth: the Happy Hotdog Klub.

You've never heard of it, I'm sure. Its name has appeared in print only once—in the last issue of the long-dead New York Herald-Tribune. Publishers know that any mention is a death sentence; not only do they avoid it, they also try to slip it into the pages of the competition. Welcome behind the looking-glass, "Dad."

The Happy Hotdog Klub was born in 1934, in the booths of "Filibusters," a posh D.C. restaurant. To avoid suspicion, the HHK cloaked itself in the jester's motley of a sophomoric, upper-class drinking society, headed by Felix Frankfurter. Other founders included Harry Hopkins, Eleanor Roosevelt, and a shadowy figure known only as "Adlai S." Though the New Deal was underway, these ur-liberals were determined to go further. They dreamed of a new America purged of the self-reliance, free enterprise, and respect for one's elders that had poisoned the well of liberty since 1776.

Phase One of HHK's master plan ran flawlessly from FDR to Carter. Historians (many of them on the payroll) call this half-century the apex of liberalism—but in reality it was a fifty-year operation to draw our enemies out into the open. Carter's precisely-calibrated weakness and dithering led to the so-called "Reagan Gambit," an attempt to discredit traditional conservatism by making its leader a nincompoop. Bush continued the ruse, adding a whiff of patrician befuddlement.

By 1992, the final piece slid into place: William Jefferson Clinton. Draft-dodging, pot-smoking, internationally-educated Clinton was HHK all the way. For example, during his governorship of Arkansas he kept prying eyes away from the Mena airport, where around

...w in tons of useless government paperwork to strangle ...sses.

...ton, the HHK anticipated ultimate victory. All signs were good: a White ...se awash in memories of the 60s, the suspiciously-independent First Lady, male aides sporting earrings, Jocelyn Elders with her frankly onanistic agenda. First would come universal health care to establish the omnipresent, grossly-overpaid bureaucracy, and then a "Work-to-Welfare" system where benefits increased exponentially based on childbearing and general irresponsibility.

But then Clinton went "rogue." As soon as Elders was dismissed (just before she announced the first-ever National Masturbation Bee), I was activated. My signal was the words "Quotas," "ACLU," and "John Lindsay" in the Times crossword puzzle.

And so, years later, I write you this letter. All is back under control; but do not look to me as a hero. The true heroes are the HHK's fearless agents provocateurs: Bob Barr, Henry Hyde, Kenneth Starr, and Linda Tripp, our much-maligned Mata Hari. And let us not forget brave Newt Gingrich, who like a phoenix was consumed but will live again. When the book of Sex-Positive True Liberalism is written, their names shall be inscribed in gold!

Soon, "Dad," we shall see the HHK's dream, the Greatest Society. It shall include:

- an all-queer military
- the abolition of the death penalty, except for smokers
- nasally-implanted radio receivers auto-tuned to NPR's "Morning Edition"
- bras outlawed and replaced with environmentally-sound mass transit
- government-subsidized anti-US dissent, at home and abroad
- the passage of a beefed-up ERA mandating unisex bathrooms, with block captains to organize all women nationwide into Sapphic covens
- a federal holiday celebrating the murder of Vincent Foster
- another federal holiday celebrating the media's cover-up of the murder of Vincent Foster
- the UN, acting under the auspices of Amnesty International, confiscating all firearms, which will be melted down and recast into statues celebrating secular humanism
- all citizens required to display bumper stickers reading "Hate is NOT a Family Value," "Visualize World Peace," and "I Reserve the Right to Arm Bears"; and, most importantly:
- the final, universal, messianic acceptance of the metric system

I must close now, "Dad"; we are pulling into Abzug Station, in our bustling capital of Kennedania, six miles below the earth's crust. For me, the "Great Game" is over. As it is for you—even now, the lethal nano-bots which coat this paper are climbing through the pores of your skin, pumping poison into your bloodstream. You understand now why no one can learn these facts and live. Think of this not as murder, but rather as taxpayer-funded euthanasia for the elderly. But during your last few seconds of consciousness,

I Remain,
Your Monica (a/k/a Frank R. Hamblen) ☐

After robbers broke into her house, tied her up, and stole her valuables, 70 year-old Evelyn Johnson dialed 911 with her tongue. After calling the police, she found the remote and channel-surfed until help arrived.

Mike
Weekend Update
1998

What is the Sound of One Hand Cramping?

Mike & Jon
Seattle Weekly
October 1999

A monk asked the Master Tungshan, "Who is the Buddha?"

Tungshan replied, "I know you are, but what am I?"

How old were you when your mother was born?

A student once asked the Sixth Patriarch, "Master, how do you get a goose out of a bottle?"

The Sixth Patriarch replied, "Add some water and yeast, and wait patiently. Soon you'll have goose beer, and after a bowl of that, there are no problems."

"Why this?" "Why that?" Stop searching in this fashion, for the truth that can be expressed in words is not the Eternal Truth. That is why toddlers are so exasperating.

When Hyakujo was with his master Baso, a flock of geese flew overhead. Seeing an opportunity to teach his disciple, Baso asked, "What is that?"

"A flock of geese," Hyakujo replied.

"Where are they flying to?" asked Baso.

"They are flying away," said Hyakujo.

Baso twisted Hyakujo's nose with great force. "You say they have flown away, but they are always overhead just the same."

Hyakujo trembled with satori [sudden enlightenment]. "So that is why you walk under an umbrella."

He who knows, does not speak. He who speaks, does not know. (Except for me now, obviously.)

Monk: "What do you say when I come to you with nothing?"
Master: "Fling it down!"
Monk: "I said I had nothing. What shall I let go?"
Master: "If so, take it away."
Monk: "Oh, I see you're in one of your moods."

What is the meaning of Bodhidharma's coming from the East? Since when could he drive?

Do not fear Death. It is merely a pause between two forms of life...the "pause that refreshes."

One sage said to the other, "The fish has flopped out of the net! How will it live?"
The other sage said, "When you have gotten out of the net, I will tell you."
The first sage said, "Wha-? Oh, it's a METAPHOR!"
Replied the second sage, "Du-uh."

The Sixth Patriarch attempted to stump his acolyte by asking, "If all things are reducible to the One, what is the One reducible to?"

The acolyte thought a moment and answered, "Buzz."

The Sixth Patriarch was well pleased, and appointed the acolyte Features Editor of Time Out.

"Does a dog have Buddha-nature?" asked the acolyte.

"That is the most important question of all," said the Master.

"So what's the answer?" asked the acolyte.

"That is also the most important question of all," said the Master.

"This is very frustrating."

"Please answer in the form of a question," said the Master.

Hiju Yesho was once asked by a monk, "What is Buddha?"

Yesho answered, "The cat is climbing up the post."

The monk confessed his inability to understand the Master.

"No matter," said Yesho. "Them cats is good eatin'."

Joshu asked the teacher Nansen, "Is death an end or a beginning?"

Nansen thought for a moment, then replied, "How badly do you want to know?"

Ying-men sat with his three disciples. He laid a fan on the ground, saying, "Without calling it a 'fan,' tell me what this is."

The first disciple said, "You couldn't call it a slop-bucket." Ying-men took up his staff and promptly drove him from the room under a hail of blows.

The second disciple picked up the fan and fanned himself. He, too, was beaten away.

The third disciple opened the fan, laid a piece of cake on it, and served it to his teacher. Ying-men beat him nearly unconscious before the disciple made it out the door.

Ying-men returned to his seat, took a bite of the cake, and said contentedly, "I can't believe this is a *religion*."

A monk asked Huang-yen, "What is laughter?"

"What is *not* laughter?" replied Huang-yen.

"Um, I don't know how to tell you this," said the monk sheepishly, "but you really don't have a very good sense of humor." □

This wasn't our only attempt at Zen-inflected humor. We also created a book proposal for The Art of Wha-?, a spoof of Sun Tzu's The Art of War This led to our discovering a brand-new koan: what is less than zero interest? (Sorry about the scan—this is the only copy of this booklet left.)

Sketch: "His Next Speech"

Mike & Jon
(commissioned by SNL, unaired)
August 1998

(OPEN ON: WHITE HOUSE MAP ROOM)

CLINTON

My fellow Americans: last Monday evening I gave a speech that no American would ever want to give – especially any American who was me. While my statements during that broadcast were legally accurate, I did not volunteer information, and I know that some of what I said gave a false impression. I misled people – even myself – and I deeply regret that.

First, let me say that I did not, as I stated, give Monday's speech from the Map Room of the White House. I was in a carefully constructed set aboard the USS Rochester, a secret stealth submarine moored at the bottom of the Potomac River. As this had no bearing on the substance of my talk on Monday, I felt it was no one's business but my own. This was an error on my part, for which I am solely and completely responsible.

(HE GESTURES)

This, of course, is the real Map Room.

Next, during my speech I repeatedly referred to "Ms. Lewinsky," which implied that (MAKING QUOTES MARKS WITH FINGERS) "she" is a woman. In fact, last week the Director of the Central Intelligence Agency informed me that, genetically-speaking, Monica Lewinsky is both male and female – what scientists call a "she-male."

You can be sure that no one was more surprised to learn this than I was. My motivations for not revealing this were to protect my family from embarrassment. I also felt this was no one's business but mine and hers. And his.

As a result of this information, I am now advised that my relationship with Ms.-slash-Mr. Lewinsky was more than inappropriate – it was also illegal in ten states, as well as Puerto Rico. To those who would criticize me for a liaison such as this, all I can say is – try it, you might like it. I know I've learned a lot about myself. While it is true that our relationship was in some ways wrong, in other ways it was oh so right.

I say again: at no time did I ask any other person to lie, to obstruct justice or conceal evidence. However, I did ask myself to do those things, and I said – "sure, what the hell." But I never expressly directed Ms.-slash-Mr. Lewinsky to keep quiet, and I find it frankly ludicrous that such a self-possessed and ambitious young person would be intimidated by the mere wishes of the President of the United States.

Actually, I lied just then. I'm not the President. I'm not sure who I am. The last thing I remember is taking a tour of the White House. I hit my head on a bust of Teddy Roosevelt, and the next thing I knew, I was in the Oval Office! I think I've done pretty good!

Incidentally, many of you have asked, will Hillary and I remain married? The answer is, we're not married. Never have been, not in any way you would recognize. It's unconventional, but you'll have to trust me when I say it's worked out great for all concerned. I don't even know her real name!

It is time – past time – to move on, to repair the ripped cocktail dress of our national discourse and erect proud new standards of America excellence. As my mother told me so many years ago, there are plenty of fish in the sea. And don't worry about Chelsea. She's an actor, and she's very well paid. The current "Chelsea XVI" is a recent immigrant from Uzbekistan and glad for the work. Everyone's A-OK here at 1600 Pennsylvania Avenue.

In closing, then, I ask you to turn away from the spectacle of the past seven months, and to prepare for the challenges facing us as a nation – for instance, my speech next week, in which I will explain why nothing I said tonight was true.

Thank you for listening, and God bless America.

(A SAILOR APPEARS IN SHOT)

SAILOR

We're ready to dive.

CLINTON
(to SAILOR)

Take 'er down.

(HE GIVES THE CAMERA HIS BEST LOOK OF SINCERITY AND DOES HIS THUMB GESTURE)

Live from New York, it's Saturday Night! ☐

On Wednesday Christian Slater reported to a suburban LA jail to serve ninety days for, among other crimes, biting a friend. In interviews Slater has said that his problems have been caused by low self-esteem. The good news is that his low self-esteem was caused by his belief that he wasn't brave enough to bite people.

Jon
Weekend Update
1998

This Monday Jodie Foster confirmed rumors that she is pregnant. Religious leaders around the world urged calm.

Mike
Weekend Update
1998

In the Next Milennium

A collar-like device worn on the throat, which allows any member of the vertebrate family to speak standard American English, will create a brief sensation. Enthusiasm will fade as it is found that animals espouse a particularly dreary form of existentialism, strong opinions about abstract art, and nothing else.

Mike
1992-99

A Singapore company will colonize the Moon; genetically-engineered dogs will be imported to produce oxygen. They will be specially trained to find travelers lost on the planet's surface, and blow into their mouths until help arrives.

A hybrid form of corn will be developed that will produce kernels in the shapes of hearts, corporate logos, and cartoon characters.

A small generator will be attached to as many birds as are catchable, to generate electricity from their flight. Suddenly, flocks of pigeons will be transformed from an annoying blight to a natural resource, and a source of civic pride.

A worldwide trend towards "more flavorful" government will lead to a brief flowering of kooks in charge. Things will go surprisingly well.

After centuries of corporate promises and high-budget commercials, the videophone will be scrapped as a lousy idea.

Art will be standardized, and created using a detailed personality test of the viewer. Artists will be completely subsidized by the government; styles of art will form important portions of the platforms of political parties.

Cattle-ranching will be made much more humane by the introduction of Black Angus cattle which lay steaks like hens do eggs.

Computers will become so efficient that they will be too annoying for most humans to use.

Cosmetics will be become so sophisticated as to make personal appearance totally fraudulent. Therefore, allure will be determined by eccentricity rather than conventional beauty.

Crayons will come 1,500 to the box, and will include colors in the UV and IR spectra.

Credit cards, debit cards and all other species of electronic money will be embedded in the fleshy rear-end of consumers, where their addition and removal will not be dangerous or difficult. Special chairs will record all purchases and payments.

Criminals will be prohibited from engaging in any virtual reality, and forced to "live outside" for a proscribed period of time. Few so punished will stray again.

Food will become digitized, making its flavor clearer, more precise, and immune to spoilage. For best results, you will have to wipe it with a special acetone-based cleaning fluid before consuming.

Glasses for animals will be common, as will wigs, glass eyes and hearing aids.

Greeting cards will able to express every possible emotion or relationship. Consequently, they will count for much of the day-to-day interaction of human beings.

Hamsters will skyrocket in popularity after it is found that a simple dietary additive makes them execrete a refreshing lager.

Harried parents will be able to outfit their children with a "cloaking device" that will enable them to be neither seen nor heard, so that the adults can achieve maximum relaxation from their ever shrinking free time.

High school will be replaced by a series of painful injections.

Historians will be devastated after a chance discovery proves that the Roman Empire was an elaborate hoax. Academic faculties will rebound by switching this discipline from History to Literature, and continuing on as if nothing had happened.

Hockey and boxing will slowly diminish in popularity, until the Leagues of both decide to merge in a last-ditch attempt to survive. No holds barred "hoxing" will provide the mix of garish uniforms and pure brutality that future sports fans hanker for.

In an effort to slow cultural plundering on the part of rich suburban teenagers, ghetto youth will speak Latin among themselves to express solidarity and distinctness.

It will be discovered that whales and dolphins, man's closest oceanic relation, have been training sharks to attack bathers for the last two centuries. Whaling and tuna-fishing, the objects of this stratagem, will skyrocket in popularity. "So you wanna fight, eh?"

Junk mail will be received from conception. Which mailing lists one is on will be the most reliable mark of social standing.

Medical science will have progressed to such a degree that people can live to be 175 years old. Few choose to, however, since it is discovered that after 100, the events of the life in question begin inexplicably repeating themselves.

Military hardware will be so small that wars will be indistinguishable from sickness, with all conflicts happening on the microscopic level. Good hygiene will be considered a matter of national security.

Movies will be discontinued after their realism reaches such heights that 35% of every audience dies of heart failure, every performance. Theaters will shut down, not willing to pay the astronomical insurance premiums; predictably, an underground industry will flourish.

People will like other people less—with many more people in the world to choose from, they can afford to be pickier. Also, the more realistic fantasies become, the more glaring people's shortcomings will become.

Pets will be animals genetically-engineered to look like popular cartoon characters or celebrities. Their diet will be supplemented with mood-altering drugs to ensure that they provide maximum comfort and companionship to their owners.

Pregnant women will be able to eat special diets to produce children of various talents and aptitudes. The widespread availability of the "Mozart diet" will make musical ineptitude quite refreshing.

Races will intermarry with such vigor that the human race will be a uniform beige. Racism, while held by some with no small measure of nostalgia, will become simply too difficult to practice.

Recreation will be perceived as a quaint relic of the past. Similar feelings of carefree release will be compressed into a much shorter time thanks to a machine that will stimulate appropriate areas of the brain.

Samples of all important, intriguing, or visually pleasing plants will be kept in plant zoos.

Scientists will solve the problem of world hunger by coming up with a way for people to harness photosynthesis via a series of harmless injections. This option will only be embraced by the lower classes, since it will be found to turn the user a shade of green that is impossible to match outfits with.

The British Royal Family will still act like idiots, but Great Britain will not get rid of them, for fear that the country would then be indistinguishable from America.

The death of US President and ladies' man John Kennedy will be conclusively proved a suicide.

The discovery of aliens will allow human beings to relax, knowing that the future of Life throughout the universe does not rest on their unstable shoulders. This good feeling will not extend to wanting your daughter to marry one.

The national anthems of all recognized countries will be combined, via computer, into one world anthem. It will be a commercial success, but a critical failure.

The weather will be completely controlled, and will be used to drive criminals insane.

Up to thirteen different sexes will be created, primarily for purposes of market research.

Widely available, harmless drugs will make sleeping unnecessary and, for most, rather difficult. Therefore, it will become an extremely popular sport.

Widespread environmental toxins will ensure that red is everyone's favorite color. ☐

Sketch: "Dr. Veegin"

Jon
August 1999

(FADE IN: A CRYSTAL SWINGING BACK AND FORTH, GLINTING IN THE LIGHT)
(SUPER: "DR. VEEGIN, LICENSED HYPNOTIST" WITH 800 NUMBER)

DR. VEEGIN
(voiceover)
You are getting sleepy…you are getting very sleepy…

(PULL BACK: TO SHOW DR. VEEGIN, STANDING NEXT TO A FIREPLACE IN A COMFORTABLE OFFICE. SOMETHING ABOUT HIM IS SLIGHTLY SHIFTY.)

DR. VEEGIN
(on-screen)
Hello, I'm Dr. Nathaniel Veegin, certified hypnotist. In the last decade, science has finally recognized the amazing power of hypnosis. Would you like to stop smoking? Lose weight? Get relief from nervous ticks? With just one visit to my office, you can make that happen with the incredible power of your own subconscious mind. But don't take my word for it – listen to what some of my patients have to say.

(PHOTOGRAPH OF PATIENT #1, A FRAZZLED LOOKING MAN WITH A CIGARETTE IN HIS MOUTH.)

PATIENT #1
(voiceover)
I used to be a four pack a day smoker. I tried to quit a hundred times.

(DISSOLVE TO: PATIENT #1 LOOKING MUCH HAPPIER, WITH HIS HANDS AT HIS SIDE OUT OF FRAME)

PATIENT #1
(on-screen)
But after just one trip to Dr. Veegin, I stopped smoking once and for all!

(HIS RIGHT HAND APPEARS IN FRAME HOLDING A LIT CIGARETTE. HE CASUALLY TAKES A DEEP DRAG AND CONTENTEDLY EXHALES)

PATIENT #1
I never thought quitting could be this easy!

(HE TAKES A DEEP DRAG.)

And the amazing thing is, I don't even crave nicotine.

(HIS OTHER HAND APPEARS IN FRAME, HOLDING THREE MORE CIGARETTES, WHICH HE PUTS IN HIS MOUTH ALONG WITH THE FIRST)

PATIENT #1
(on-screen)
Thanks, Dr. Veegin!

(INSERT: PHOTOGRAPH OF PATIENT #2, A HARRIED LOOKING WOMAN WITH A LOOK OF ANGUISH ON HER FACE)

PATIENT #2
(voiceover)
I used to have terrible Obsessive-Compulsive Disorder that made me count up to seven after every sentence I said, and when I stopped talking, hit myself on the head and make a silly sound...

(DISSOLVE TO: PATIENT #2, ALSO MUCH HAPPIER)

PATIENT #2
(on-screen)
...but one trip to Dr. Veegin, and I'm cured!
(quickly, to self)
One-two-three-four-five-six-seven.
(to camera)
It's so great to be normal again!
(to self)
One-two-three-four-five-six-seven.
(to camera)
Thanks, Dr. Veegin!
(to self)
One-two-three-four-five-six-seven.
(hitting herself on the head)
Boop! Boop!

(INSERT: PHOTOGRAPH OF PATIENT #3, AN EXTREMELY OBESE MAN IN A CAFTAN)

PATIENT #3
(voiceover)
This is me, six months ago. I was fat and miserable.

(DISSOLVE TO: CLOSE UP ON SMILING FACE OF PATIENT #3)

PATIENT #3
(on-screen)
But after just one appointment with Dr. Veegin, I lost over a

hundred pounds, and never once felt hungry. So this is me, today!

(HE GESTURES EXUBERANTLY AS THE CAMERA QUICKLY PULLS BACK TO SHOW HIS FULL BODY, STILL EXTREMELY OBESE, BUT NOW WEARING A TEENY-TINY SPEEDO)

PATIENT #3 (cont'd)

Thanks, Dr. Veegin!

(CUT TO: DR. VEEGIN IN FRONT OF FIREPLACE)

DR. VEEGIN

Hypnosis can do this for you too...even in the toughest cases, where regular medical treatment offers no hope.

(INSERT: MUGSHOT OF A ROUGH-LOOKING DR. VEEGIN WITH A MOUSTACHE)

DR. VEEGIN

(voiceover)

I used to be a con artist who pretended to be a doctor. Back then, I used my gift for hypnosis to make desperate people think that their problems were gone, when really they were just as bad as ever.

(DISSOLVE TO: DR. VEEGIN, NOW THE WELL-GROOMED DOCTOR)

DR. VEEGIN

(onscreen)

But using self-hypnosis I gained the discipline to become a real doctor who helps people solve their problems for real.

(PULL BACK: TO SHOW DR. VEEGIN IS STANDING WITH NUMEROUS PATIENTS, INCLUDING NUMBERS 1-3 AND SEVERAL OTHERS, ONE AN ELDERLY MAN DRESSED AS A BALLERINA AND ONE IN A SUIT OF ARMOR)

ALL

Thanks, Dr. Veegin!

(CUT TO: A CRYSTAL SWINGING BACK AND FORTH, GLINTING IN THE LIGHT)

(SUPER: "DR. VEEGIN, LICENSED HYPNOTIST" WITH 800 NUMBER)

DR. VEEGIN

(voiceover)

You believe you are getting sleepy...you truly believe you are getting very sleepy.

OUT. □

The Periodic Table

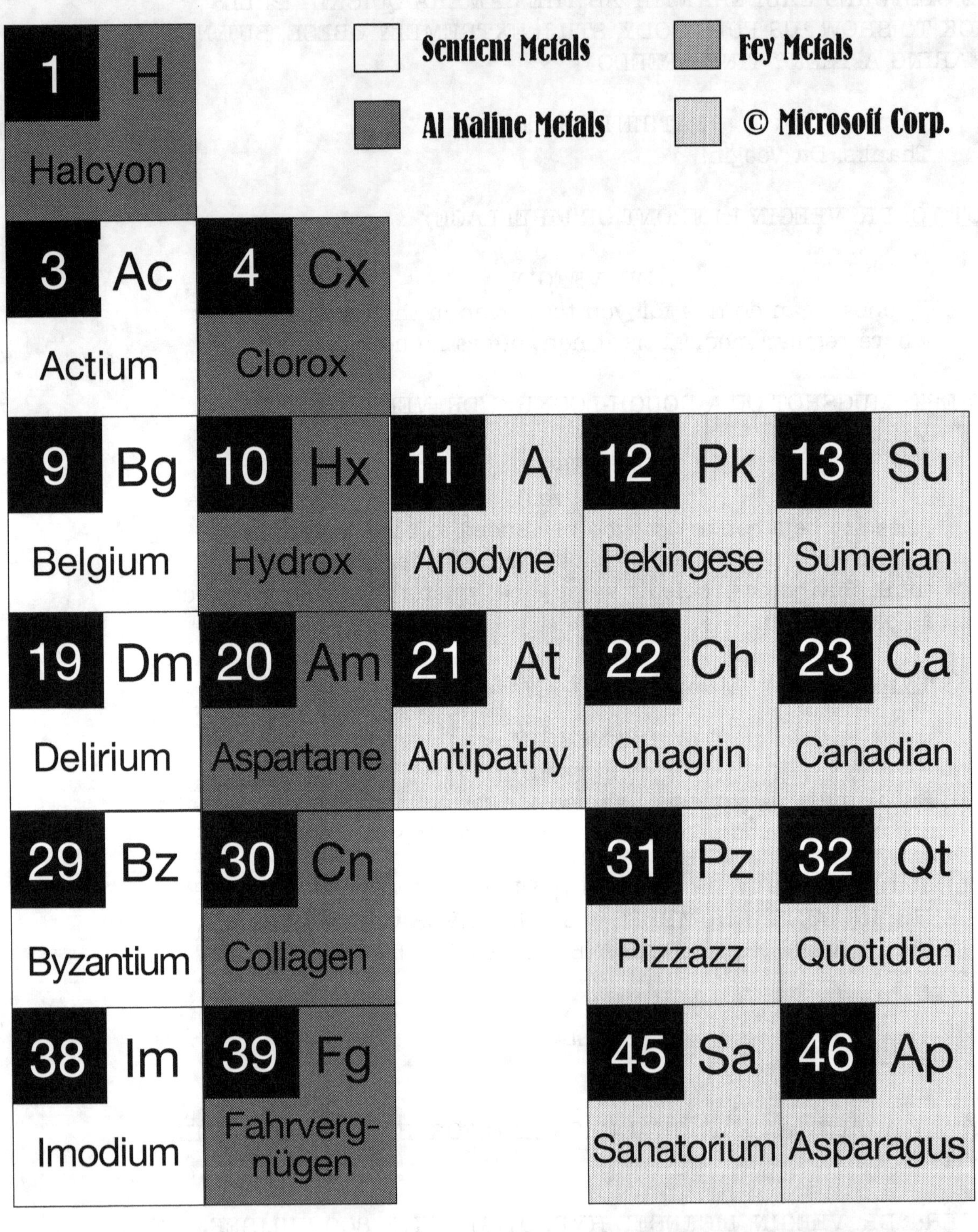

Mike & Jon
The Atlantic Monthly
August 1999

# of Rejected Elements

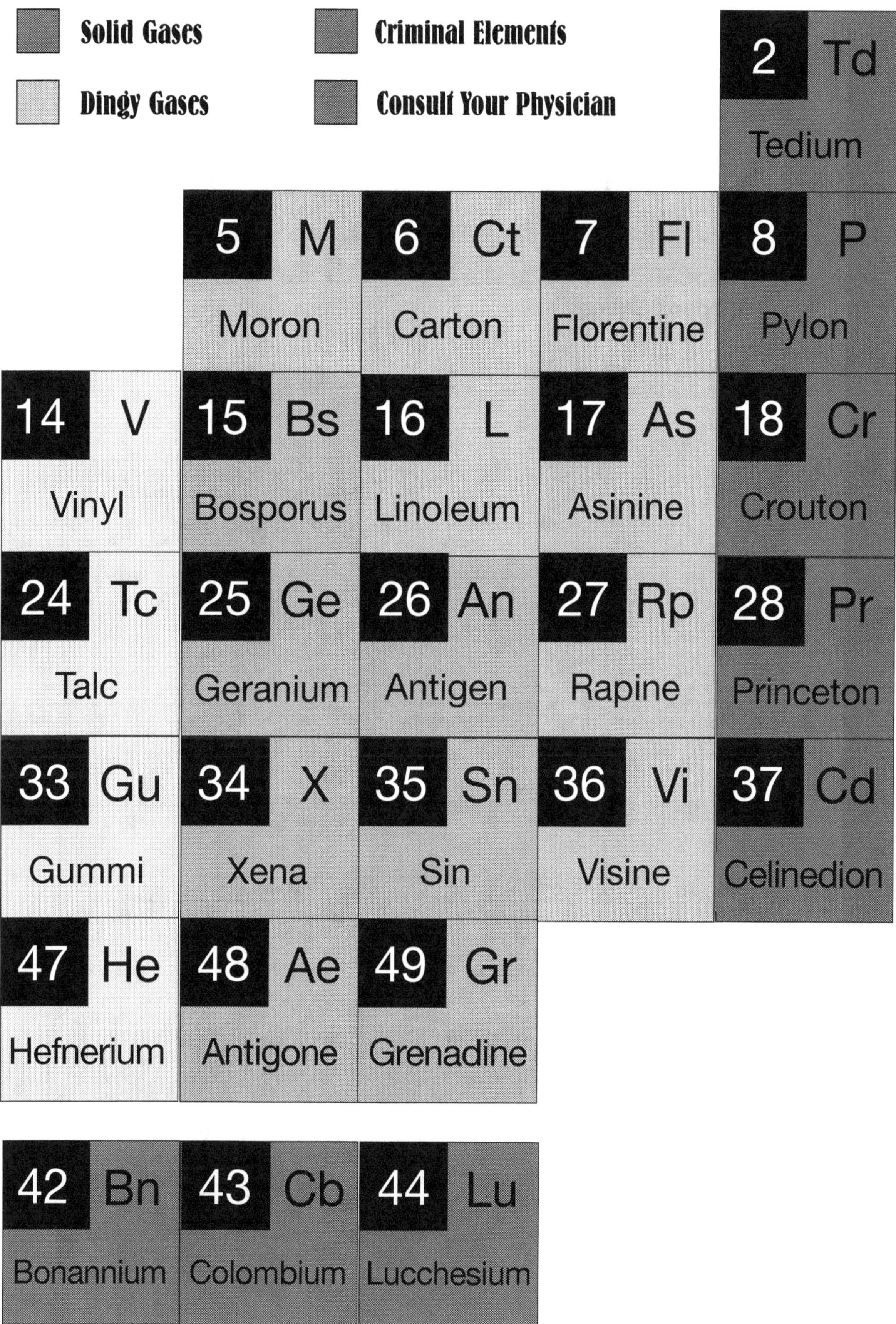

Mike
some alt-weekly in Ohio I think
early 2001

Decision '04

brought to you by

Hello, **Jane Q. Smith**! Today is **Tuesday, November 3, 2004**.

I am not Jane. You have **610** VoteBux in your account. Spend

☑ Flip-flop Finder™ is **ON**. ☑ ChadZap™ **ACTIVATED**.
☑ MuckBot™ is **ON**. Your Paper of Record: NY Times

The President of the United States 2004

(Time Left to Vote: 00 days 12 hours 13 min)

George W. Bush	**Albert Gore, Jr.**
Richard Cheney	Hillary Rodham Clinton
Republican	**Democrat**
100 VoteBux	100 VoteBux
For those who like a relaxed fit to their Chief Executive, we present an update of a classic. Our new George Bush has twice as much of the moneyed, inarticulate charm of the original, to provide four-season, full-term, pre-broken-in comfort. With Bush, the leadership goes in before the name goes on!	Achieve total representation with this powerful, no-nonsense advocate for your well-being. Hand-buffed and lovingly neutered, Al Gore doesn't clash with any lifestyle/religion, from Baptist to Buddhist. Dependable toughness and unbeatable quality come together in one painstakingly-crafted statesman. Go Gore in '04!
Vote Recount (Please vote only ONCE.)	Vote Recount (Please vote only ONCE.)
Search for "Skull and Bones collectibles" on Ebay	Buy the "Lil' Al" officially-licensed home fuel cell at HomeDepot.com
Bush Review of the Day (write an online review and share your opinions with other voters)	**Gore Review of the Day** (write an online review and share your opinions with other voters)
GOPchick23@mindstring.com writes: it was the happiest day of my life when justice scallia named W president and iam honored to vote for him again.he kept us strong and showed those people who thought that he was too stupid. who's laughing now, trinidad/tobago?--our "sacred honor" is BACK!! i enjoyed the "W-mentary" on the history channel. if he executed you, you probably did it, and even if you didn't, you probably did something else that you got away with. anyway, God will sort it all out in His good time.	**swilentz@princeton.edu** writes: Lieberman's simultaneous chairmanship of the DNC and RNC raises questions, but to claim there are no differences between the parties is absurd. Vide: during the Bush Presidency, distinguished historians have been invited to the White House so infrequently that it poses a clear and present danger to the Republic. Gore's faults aside, a vote for Jello Biafra *is* a vote for Bush. And it's demagoguery at its worst to call Hillary a "carpetbagger" just because of her recent move to West Palm Beach.
Ask This Candidate a Question: Ask Did Trinidad REALLY attack	Ask This Candidate a Question: Ask Who killed Ralph Nader?
Special Offers for Bush voters from: the XFL, Fox News, Charles Schwab, Amway...many more	Special Offers for Gore voters from: Slim-Fast, Dreamworks, Red Herring, Todd Gitlin, more

Can't find what you're looking for? Search our database of Marginal Political Parties NEW!

Have you heard about AutoVote, our new personal voting service? After entering your voting history onto our secure server, AutoVote translates the positions of your preferred politicians into numerical values. Then it uses complex algorithms to choose the candidate you'd most likely vote for, in every race, all the time, EVERYWHERE. Our Suffragebot® is constantly scanning for elections, so you'll be sure to make your voice heard again and again. Sign up before Dec. 1 and receive $500 from Ameritrade!

Ready to Spend Your VoteBux? Our Mall of Democracy Is OPEN!

Register a Friend and Get a Limited-Edition "Sam the Eagle" Beanie Baby!

Suspect vote fraud? Email our webmaster.
This website en Español.
© 2001-2004, Democracy.com.
Democracy.com is a publicly-traded company listed on the NASDAQ: DEMO.

What Falwell REALLY Meant

"I really believe that the pagans, and the abortionists, and the feminists, and the gays and the lesbians...the A.C.L.U., People for the American Way, all of them who have tried to secularize America, I point the finger in their face and say, 'You helped this happen.'"

—Jerry Falwell, September 13th, 2001, on "The 700 Club" about last week's terrorist attacks

"I sincerely regret that comments I made...were taken out of their context."

—Jerry Falwell, September 14th

Mike & Jon
Village Voice.com
September 21, 2001

Nine Possible Contexts:

1. "...NOT."

2. "You know, I'm really high right now, so this may not make any sense, but..."

3. "Keeping in mind that today is Opposites Day, I emphasize that..."

4. "My son showed me this cool thing on Alta Vista, where you type something in English and then have the computer translate it into French and then into Spanish and then into German and then back to English -- it's kinda like 'Telephone,' you know? -- and something that made sense at the beginning will come out sounding like..."

5. "If an infinite number of monkeys typed on an infinite number of typewriters, one of them would write..."

6. "I want to take a break from the grim events of this week, and salute the brave people who've spent years making America a better and more tolerant place. Who's done this, who's helped this happen? Well, I'll tell you:"

7. "An insane man off camera is pointing a gun at my head and forcing me to read this statement. Quote,..."

8. "Please join me in praying that, in the wake of this horrific tragedy, Christ's message of peace will prevail, our entire country can unite in compassion, not aggression, and that no misguided person will state..."

9. "I truly believe that if Osama bin Laden had been born in America, right now he'd be saying..." □

Khmer Rouge leader Pol Pot was cremated this week on a pyre of wood and tires. Cambodians as far as eight miles away were heard to ask, "Do you smell Pot?"

Jon
Weekend Update
1998

A Message From the New York City Tourism Board

Mike & Jon
October 2001

New York City is back! Broadway is singing, the Yankees are winning, and the greatest city on earth is open for business! If you've ever wanted to visit, the Big Apple says, "Welcome!"

Except for terrorists. Terrorists, please don't come here anymore. Why not go somewhere else? Here are some suggestions, courtesy of the New York City Tourism Board.

Poorly defended and historically hostile to Islam, the quaint desert town of ALBUQUERQUE hosts an annual balloon race—which would attract substantial media attention while plunging from the sky in flames! Albuquerque's thriving arts community would be sure to immortalize your act in Guernica-like tableaus for decades to come!

Angry at freedom and modernity? Why not consider a "dirty nuke" in beautiful downtown CLEVELAND? Not only is it home to the Hall of Fame of Rock 'n' Roll, the lustful music that sets the hips of sluttish western women gyrating, it is also the setting of the alcohol-positive sitcom "The Drew Carey Show."

Yes, the east coast is terrified—but can America truly be said to be "full of fear from East to West" without an attack on ANCHORAGE? Not only does this Alaskan city host a heavy population of infidel Eskimos, its water system was named "worst guarded" by Taliban Monthly. Smallpox grants are available from the New York City Mayor's Office, his name be praised!

BOCA RATON, well-known as the Winter Headquarters for International Jewry, was recently named "America's Hypochondria Capital" by Fortune. And why not? Nobody's more sensitive to slight flu-like symptoms than a Zionist snowbird! Just one Pennysaver sprinkled with baby powder is sure to cause a massive panic. They swamp the city's infrastructure, and pass the savings on to you!

Antebellum charm meets absolute vulnerability in lovely SAVANNAH, where a notoriously incompetent Mayor and fractious City Council wait to collapse at the merest touch of terror. Add demoralized, underpaid law enforcement, and you've got Paradise here on Earth! Use our coupon to receive 25% off on cropduster rental before January 15th! □

Jon
Weekend Update
1998

In China, supermarket tabloids are saying Monica Lewinsky was a KGB agent trained from childhood to seduce the President. The papers said swimmer Greg Louganis was also in the program, just in case Barney Frank was elected.

After a severe ice storm last January, officials in New York predicted that there would be huge batch of newborns this October. But there weren't, so the doctors are calling it "the most frigid ice storm on record."

Mike & Jon
Weekend Update
1998

A Nevada woman whose son committed suicide last week, has had her dead son's sperm frozen, so that she can find an egg donor, have the embryo implanted, and bear her own grandchildren. Ironically, the boy's note said, "I'm finally free of you, you controlling bitch."

Jon
Weekend Update
1998

Following the recent launch of a missile by North Korea, the United States and Japan have agreed to conduct joint research on a defense system. This is that system. [picture of Godzilla]

Mike
Weekend Update
1998

Sketch: "The Little-Known Constitution"

Mike & Jon
WNYC
February, 2002

HOST

Since 9/11, there's been a lot in the news about what seem to be the Bush administration's unique interpretations of the Constitution. But experts say America's founding document is actually quite different from what many believe. Here's NPR's Marly Itzy, in Washington.

ITZY

"Unreasonable searches and seizures." "Due process of law." All Americans know these famous phrases from the Constitution. Unless they're from the Declaration of Independence.

But if you haven't been reading the paper carefully, you might be surprised how much the Constitution has changed since you took high school civics. Here's Yale Law professor Harold Weisberg.

WEISBERG

Well, the history is hazy. It's hard to tell exactly what happened, because ever since the passage of the 38th Amendment in the late eighties, nothing Congress does has to be written down. But it seems that one night Congress and the State Legislatures entered a radio station contest to see who could pass the most constitutional amendments in the next eight hours.

ITZY

And so the United States Congress, galvanized by the lure of free tickets to Oingo Boingo, passed hundreds of amendments in a booze and coffee-filled all-nighter, reshaping American democracy at a single shaky stroke. Legislators who were there still call it "Black Sunday"...adding, "Not for us, of course. For YOU."

WEISBERG

Even since then military tribunals have been, constitutionally speaking, absolutely fine. You have to remember the Constitution is a living document. I think of it less like a piece of paper, and more like a Bengal tiger: it's really cute when it's a baby, but when it grows up it will rip you into pieces and eat you. That's why I'm calling my next book, "How to Protect Yourself and Your Loved Ones From the U.S. Constitution."

ITZY

Majorie Perkins was Solicitor General during the Carter administration. She says several amendments make it unlikely the Supreme Court will strike down any of President Bush's initiatives.

PERKINS

For instance, there's the 42nd Amendment, which reads, "Section I: In times of national tribulations, the government shall be absolutely forbidden from playing on the fears of the people in such a way as to extend or deepen its power, or to nullify or abrogate the rights customarily enjoyed by the governed. Section II: NOT!!!"

ITZY

Even if the Justices wanted to talk action against the Executive Branch, says Perkins, they might not be able to.

PERKINS

Most important in this respect in the 92nd Amendment, which reads: "Separation of powers is merely a figure of speech and shouldn't be taken literally."

ITZY

But not everyone agrees with Perkins. Professor Weisberg says there may be upcoming court challenges based on Amendments 500 and up, which is the point he believes Congress broke into the Jägermeister.

WEISBERG

I'm thinking specifically of the 502nd Amendment, which reads: "The American people would like to wish Senator Bob Haskins luck on his upcoming knee surgery. Good luck, Bob!"

Then there's Amendment 612: "Every U.S. citizen must own an ocelot." Amendment 613: "Ocelot, noun, a nocturnal wildcat of South America, having a greyish-yellow coat with black spots." And Amendment 614: "Every U.S. citizen must own a dictionary so that Congress doesn't have to look everything up for them ALL THE DAMN TIME."

ITZY

Whatever happens, one thing is certain: the U.S. Constitution is not what it once was. Nothing shows this more clearly than the 1000th and currently final Amendment: "Section I: The Constitution of the United States is hereby declared unconstitutional. Section II: Suck on THAT, James Madison!"

In Washington, I'm Marly Itzy.

(OUT) □

A Declaration of Independence

Mike & Jon
June 2002

The unanimous Declaration of the world's Normal People (we know who we are), When in the Course of human events, it becomes necessary for the Normal People of this Planet to dissolve the political bands which have connected them with their Leaders, and to give getting along without Leaders a real Shot, courtesy requires that we should declare the causes of this long-overdue separation, just so we're all on the same page.

We hold these truths to be self-evident, that all Leaders are a pretty dodgy proposition -- That even the best ones are Self-Absorbed Primadonnas, and the rest are seriously Craze-o Lunatics – That Normal People have the right to tell their Leaders "see Ya, wouldn't want to be Ya" -- That to secure this right of being left alone, we should set up a special Island to which all Leaders can be sent, so that they can bicker, and posture, and pursue the Phantom of Eternal Fame amongst themselves without Injuring all the rest of us -- That this Island could maybe, this is just off the top of our heads you understand, be like Epcot Center, with the whole world in miniature so the Leaders could conquer it and lose it and bend it to their Mighty Will and lose it again, and generally Ruin It to their hearts' content, without bothering Us. Prudence indeed will dictate that the long-established Idea of having Leaders should not be changed for light or transient Causes, but, come on. We've given this concept plenty of Time, at least 8,000 years, and it's for the birds. To prove this, let Facts be submitted to a candid world.

The world's Leaders have somehow convinced us that we are all on different Teams, sort of, and that they are the rightful captains of these Teams.

They have tried to weld us together by constantly harping on our Team's Great and Glorious Destiny, assuming that we, like them, give a shit. In lower voices, they assure us that we will be in Big Trouble if we don't do exactly as they Say.

They have persuaded us to try to kill members of the other Teams, instead of following our natural instinct, which is to indulge our curiosity about whether people from different countries have discovered any new Sex Tricks, or have Better Food.

They have gotten us to go on ludicrously dangerous missions against the other Teams, while they remain safely behind at their Impregnable Mountain Redoubts. This has insured that the people responsible for starting Wars always survive, and can't wait to start the Next One.

They have started innumerable, catastrophic conflicts to, for example, impress some Girl that rejected them in High School, or to prove to their Mother that they're just as successful as their Older Brother. Read their Biographies if you don't believe Us.

They've informed us that they've talked to God, and that He agrees with them Completely.

They have our laws so complicated that, while we know we're being Screwed, we can never figure out Exactly How.

They think that we're Fascinated by them, despite the fact that, by steadily reducing our voting rate for The past fifty years, we keep giving them a resolute and obvious Hint.

They have proven, once and for all, that you can be extremely dangerous and extremely boring at the same time.

In every stage of these Oppressions we have humbly petitioned for redress by bitching among ourselves, reading the paper with a weary cynicism, and laughing at the opening monologues on late night television. We have even allowed Dennis Miller on Monday Night Football. The cost is finally too dear, and we need a new Strategy.

We, therefore, the Normal People of this Planet, who don't care who's on the money, or think that anybody will (or should) remember any of us in 500 years, do solemnly publish and declare that all the world's Leaders are hereby relieved of their positions; that our feeling is, enough already with the Jihads and the Crusades and Glorious Struggles and Finest Hours; that we believe we will be much better off without them, relying for our safety instead on our inability to organize a three-person trip to 7-Eleven, much less sustained armed conflict; that it's time to get this Leader Island idea off the ground; that if, once the Leaders have been sent to the Island, any of us develop Leader-tendencies, we will encourage such Persons to develop a Hobby, or get them a Date with somebody Nice, and this will help them remember what's important. And for the support of this Declaration, with a firm reliance on the protection of divine Providence we mutually pledge to each other our Lives, our Fortunes and our dearest Hope that we can finally get some Peace and Quiet. We are not Kidding. □

Letters to the Editor

Jon
late 2001

Dear Editor:
Your paper has published little coverage of the House of Representatives' recent "stimulus" bill, which forks over $25 billion to huge corporations—most notably Enron, one of President Bush's largest campaign donors. This bill is a transparent attempt to bilk a distracted public.

I am outraged. I demand that you publish absolutely no coverage of the bill, and use the extra space to tell us more about anthrax. Should I hoard Cipro, or doxycycline? What's the difference between inhaled and cutaneous? Are there other, even worse kinds? Could there be? And, what about Eastern Equine Encephalitis?

As someone who is neither famous nor a mail carrier, my risk of catching anthrax is infinitesimal. So I rely on your thrice-daily "Anthrax Attacks America" email updates to keep me in a state of low-level hysteria. It's been said before, but bears repeating: America will never win the war on terrorism unless the media devote all their resources to rumor-mongering and ill-informed, panicky speculation.

Jacob Huuurn
Nebraska, Ohio

Dear Sir/Madam:
I am writing in regards to your article, "President Signs Anti-Terrorist Measure" (page 16, column 2, bottom). Rushed through in the heat of the moment, the USA Patriot Act has serious implications for all Americans: law enforcement authorities will now be able to enter and search citizens' homes without a warrant, even in cases unconnected to terrorism. Some have called this "the greatest infringement on civil liberties since the Civil War," and I, for one, find it hard to disagree.

Fortunately, I've been distracted by your exciting coverage of Harry Potter and the Sorcerer's Stone! I especially enjoyed the eight-part story about AOL Time Warner's super-savvy, low-key marketing strategy. Also noteworthy was your roundtable discussion on whether Harry's scar should have been in the middle of his forehead rather than to the side. And finally, though I've heard it all before, J.K. Rowling's life story was as inspiring as ever.

I am pleased to say that I've now forgotten what the beginning of this letter was about. Keep up the good work!

Nancy Person
Utah, Utah

To the Editors:
Now more than ever, America needs responsible, informed debate about the choices in front of our nation.

I therefore commend your columnists for using recent, incredibly traumatizing events to grind the same old axes. It's comforting to know that, no matter what happens in the real world, the mighty river of truth-owning, sectarian bloviation flows on!

Lucy van Pelt (I know, I know)
Ontario, Alabama

To Whom It May Concern:
I am currently a refugee in Afghanistan. As you know, there is a very real chance of mass starvation in our country this winter, with as many as five million Afghans dead. We are facing one of the greatest humanitarian disasters of modern times. Luckily, it is still preventable.

So, my family and myself are wondering: what's the latest with Oprah and Jonathan Franzen?

(no signature) □

This week the U.S. Navy named its newest Seawolf attack submarine the "USS Jimmy Carter." They'd planned to name it after Bill Clinton, but they didn't want to hear all the jokes about it being long, hard, and full of seamen.

Mike
Weekend Update
1998

Tuesday, two executives of the Columbia House Record & Tape Club were killed in an Indiana car crash. It seems God forgot to check off the little box saying he didn't want them to be sent to Him automatically.

Jon
Weekend Update
1998

Scientists are conducting DNA testing on blood from the mysterious Shroud of Turin. They're hoping to match it to a communion wafer.

Mike
Weekend Update
1998

Why the _____s Hate the _____s

A Pocket Guide to Religious and Ethnic Strife Throughout All Human History

Mike & Jon
Village Voice.com
May 9, 2002

1. They stole our _______!

2. At the Battle of _______ in the __th century, they used unfair tactics to defeat us. We cannot rest until the souls of our dead are avenged.

3. Their religion is absurd. Offensive, really—did you know they actually believe _______? And they won't be happy until *everybody* believes it!

4. While it may not be "politically correct" to say so, science has proven them to be _______.

5. They smell weird.

6. They live like animals. Children, education, the future—none of these matter to them.

7. Their music is primitive, and encourages people to _______.

8. Can you believe they eat _______? Think about that for a second—they actually put _______ *in their mouths.*

9. They want to sully our women.

10. There are so many of them—all they do is _______! If we're not careful, someday soon we'll be submerged beneath a flood of _______!

11. If there's anything worse than a _________, it's a _________-lover. These traitors are trying to destroy us from within.

12. Sure, there are a few good _________s. But better safe than sorry.

13. Yes, we killed ________ of them. You can't expect them to understand it was in self-defense—they're totally irrational. Sooner or later, they will seek revenge, and when they do, we must be prepared to kill more. That's the only language they understand.

14. Of course we seem prejudiced. The media is obviously pro-_______.

15. *They're* the reason we're so unhappy. □

Last weekend a boy scout was struck by a stray bullet while on a camping trip with his troop. In response, the Boy Scouts of America say they will change their slogan from "Be Prepared" to "Be Prepared To Die."

Jon
Weekend Update
1998

The trustees of Harvard said yesterday they will take legal action against any unauthorized use of the Harvard name. So it looks like curtains for Times Square's famous "Harvard University Sex Emporium."

Jon
Weekend Update
1998

This week Pope John Paul once again reminded Catholics that the Church forbids the use of birth control. The Pope explained that God hasn't liked contraceptives ever since the Holy Ghost's condom broke.

Mike
Weekend Update
1998

France's Supreme Court has confirmed that it will not extradite 60s-era guru Ira Einhorn, who has been indicted for murder in Pennsylvania. Einhorn is wanted for the 1977 killing of his own ego.

Mike
Weekend Update
1998

More and more fertility clinics are placing classified ads for human eggs at Ivy League schools, in hopes of getting donors with high intelligence. Representatives of these schools deny that this is the only way their students can reproduce.

Mike
Weekend Update
1998

A new book out lists the top 1000 most important people of this millennium. In the top ten are Gutenberg, Columbus, Shakespeare and Darwin. C'mon-- "Police Academy" wasn't *that* good.

Mike
Weekend Update
1998

The children's television show "Zoom" is returning to PBS after 20 years. Great—just when you got that song out of your head.

Mike
Weekend Update
1998

President Clinton is awarding outgoing German Chancellor Helmut Kohl the Medal of Freedom for "changing the course of history." And "for not starting any more wars."

Jon
Weekend Update
1998

According to a USA Today poll, most American teens admit to lying and cheating, and nearly half say they've stolen something. But remember, they could be lying.

Mike & Jon
Weekend Update
1998

Heir Jordan

Mike & Jon
The Wall Street Journal
January 2000

Now that Michael Jordan has returned to the National Basketball Association, the real question is clear: will Mr. Jordan the manager enjoy anywhere near the success of Mr. Jordan the player? Probably not. One athlete, even one as intelligent, driven and incomparably gifted as Mr. Jordan, cannot turn a team like the Washington Wizards into winners.

But maybe five of him could. That is why we urge the immediately cloning of Mr. Jordan, in bulk, with the greatest possible speed. John F. Kennedy once committed the U.S. to putting a man on the moon; we believe that today's America could embody the same spirit of adventure by making lots of copies of Mr. Jordan.

To be sure, we are not scientists. We're just—well, what's the *opposite* of scientists? But we do know that once a technology is available, it is almost impossible to prevent its use. So the question is not whether an NBA star is cloned, but when—and most importantly, who?

It would be a tragedy if this technology were used to replicate another, less talented retiree like ex-Knick Kiki Vanderweghe. We mean no disrespect to Mr. Vanderweghe when we say that a duplicate of him would have no effect except to confuse his wife. Cloning Mr. Jordan, on the other hand, would have economic benefits for all of us. A study in Fortune magazine determined that Mr. Jordan has added $10 billion in value to the U.S. economy. What if, for the good of the country, Mr. Jordan gave the Federal Reserve permission to hold several hundred Jordan in case of emergency? If the market entered a period of steep decline, the Fed could distribute one Jordan to each company listed on Standard & Poor's 500, buoying its stock price and preventing calamity. A rising tide of Jordans would lift all boats.

Then there are the social benefits of cloning Mr. Jordan. Imagine the difference an army of Jordan clones would make for our troubled youth—as coaches, big brothers, math tutors. Given Mr. Jordan's worldwide celebrity, his simulacra could be dispatched to the world's hot spots at a moment's notice, transforming potential conflicts into so many autograph sessions and impromptu basketball clinics.

Biotechnicians should be allowed to incorporate Mr. Jordan's genetic material into other products. Monsanto claims that with Mr. Jordan's genes, its scientists could produce a kiwi fruit that, although bald, would have an indomitable "will to win." Others believe Mr. Jordan's uncanny jumping ability should be spliced into rice, to make the world's most important staple literally leap from the paddy into your hand. This labor-saving innovation would transform Asian societies, giving newly prosperous farmers more time to play basketball and buy Jordan-endorsed goods, creating what economists call a virtuous circle.

Of course, there will always be fear-mongering Luddites who say that man should not play God. Our retort: since God isn't playing anymore, why not have him help humanity? As Aldous Huxley wrote: "Good Lord, can't *anyone* here make a free throw?" (*Brave New World*, Unabridged Edition, 1934). We could be, quite literally, a hair away from a bright new age of peace, progress and better basketball. Isn't it worth a shot? □

Heir Jordans

Mike & Jon
2001

On February 8, 2000, in these pages, we put forth a notion startling in its audacity, but founded on clear-eyed common sense: America must clone Michael Jordan. If the cloning of a human is inevitable, we asked, shouldn't said human be a figure beloved worldwide who has added $10 billion in value to the U.S. economy?

We anticipated a flood of support and investment. Unfortunately—although we were flattered by the immediate response from Mr. Jordan's legal representatives and security personnel—this failed to materialize, and our day of celebration became one of confusion and recrimination. After much thought, we realized our mistake: we should have introduced our proposal in a better-known newspaper, with a readership more interested in business.

Nevertheless, Mr. Jordan's recent unretiring has made this concept more relevant than ever. If Mr. Jordan is going to play again, how can it possibly be fair for one team to monopolize him? The only solution is to make lots of Mr. Jordans, fast. We may be foolish to choose the same forum as before to air our views, but after lengthy debate, we concluded that there is no other U.S. publication where it is as easy to sneak into the typesetting room.

We admit that—now as then—we are not scientists. Indeed, we are less so today than we used to be, if that is possible. Small-minded people may use this fact to cast aspersions on the very idea of cloning Mr. Jordan. We will not dignify such ad hominem attacks with a response. What the world needs now isn't more petty bickering, but more Michael Jordan. We will not stop until there is, to borrow a phrase, "a Jordan in every garage."

Some point out that the past seventeen months have revealed certain technical problems with cloning. For example, according to the literature, clones "often have short lives and are grossly oversized." The first concern can be waved aside; we are talking about an athlete with legendary powers of recovery, and there is no reason to expect that his clones would be any different. The second problem is actually a benefit: a "grossly oversized" Jordan is a coach's dream, able to post up opponents like Shaquille O'Neal with ease. And if the Jordans are getting too big, perhaps they can stunt their growth by smoking extra cigars.

The other persistent question we are asked is this: will Mr. Jordan be harmed? Absolutely not. Massive "Jordan farms" pumping out thousands of copies a day can be established without him even knowing about it! In fact, it may be better if he doesn't know about it. In our experience, Mr. Jordan grows testy when approached about this idea, even when someone has taken the time to hide in the shower of his hotel suite. And while Mr. Jordan, like all of us, sheds millions of cells every day, we caution anyone from trying to take any from him. Even at 38, Mr. Jordan is one of the world's most conditioned athletes and can effortlessly elude or pummel you as he chooses. Sometimes he chooses both.

However, what he doesn't know won't hurt him. And since he is returning because of his love of the game, isn't it selfish for us to prevent clones from experiencing that love? We therefore urge all concerned citizens to send any genetic material of Mr. Jordan's that you might have lying around the house—a razor he once used, a nailclipper, a sweaty sock—to us, care of this newspaper. We will then forward this material to the appropriate scientists, and production will begin. It is, as Mr. Jordan himself might say, a "slam-dunk." □

Sketch: "Morning Announcements"

SFX: A CHIME, THEN A SLIGHTLY STIFF, MUFFLED MALE VOICE COMES OVER THE INTERCOM.

Mike & Jon
2002

PRINCIPAL:

Good morning, students, this is Principal Panopticon with today's announcements. I'm very happy and proud to report that, as of last Friday, we here at Leavenworth High have completed an entire week of school with <u>no</u> casualties.

I know what you're thinking -- soon the snooze alarm will go off and I will wake up from this wonderful dream. And I'll have to get up and go to school, where they'll be hosing down the halls and composing tributes for the yearbook. As usual.

But no -- this is no dream! We have gone a full five days with not ten, not twenty-seven, but <u>zero</u> deaths on school property. That's some kind of restraint and maturity, folks. Let's give ourselves a hand!

SFX: APPLAUSE

PRINCIPAL:

That applause <u>was</u> computer-generated, but I think that's the type of enthusiasm you would have demonstrated had you not each been bound, gagged and all-tasered-up by our school's ever-vigilant security personnel. Let's give the security folks a hand!

SFX: MORE APPLAUSE

PRINCIPAL:

That's great...To serve and protect...A lot of them are alumni, you know.

SFX: APPLAUSE CONTINUES

PRINCIPAL:

Okay, that's too much.

SFX: APPLAUSE CUTS OFF ABRUPTLY

PRINCIPAL:

It has come to my attention that some of you don't like our new school uniforms. I am well aware that many of you like to express yourselves through your clothing—but bright orange rip-stop nylon jumpsuits do that. They say, "I am a proud student/inmate of Leavenworth High! I am visible even from a helicopter!"

So they're staying.

Also here to stay are the microchips implanted at the base

of your skull. Not only do they allow our GPS satellites to keep track of you, they also have a handy disciplinary feature.

Like a Shower Massage, this feature has several settings, starting at a pleasant tingling--

SFX: QUIET BUZZING

PRINCIPAL:

--all the way up to what we call the "Ben Franklin Special."

SFX: EXTREMELY LOUD BUZZING

PRINCIPAL:

(with some relish)

Once again, that's the "Ben Franklin Special."

SFX: EXTREMELY LOUD BUZZING

PRINCIPAL:

What I find amazing about this system is that it's entirely voice-activated. All I have to do is say "a pleasant tingling"--

SFX: QUIET BUZZING

PRINCIPAL:

or, if I prefer, the "Ben Franklin Spec...

[PRINCIPAL pauses.]

PRINCIPAL

--ial."

SFX: EXTREMELY LOUD BUZZING, FOLLOWED BY APPLAUSE

PRINCIPAL:

Thank you. Glad you like it. It's not cheap, but as I always say, "Leavenworth students deserve the very best."

SFX: SMALL ALARM WHOOP

PRINCIPAL:

Uh, could the foam crew go to Mrs. Olsen's homeroom? The sensors indicate that several students there have caught on fire.

Now: last week you all took eighty-four standardized tests. There will be many more, but we just wanted to ease you into it. I'm pleased to report that slowly but surely, with lower and lower voltage, your scores are improving. For the first time in Leavenworth's history, a majority of our student/inmates have been rated -- and I quote -- "below average."

Give yourselves a hand. I'll do it for you.

SFX: APPLAUSE

PRINCIPAL (Cont'd):

Of course, this wasn't all about the shock-implants. Over the summer, we stopped using the World War I-era solvent we used to use to clean all the floors. Apparently, whenever you inhale it, it triggers a series of tiny strokes in your brain. What this means is: there's no more excuses. Let's do even better this week.

While we're on the subject, any angst-ridden loners out there planning to go on a rampage—you know who you are—are asked to please cull those students who consistently under-perform on standardized tests. A list of acceptable victims is available in my office. Express your adolescent rage and help the school out at the same time. It's the right thing to do.

OPPOSITE
Mike & Jon
2004

Just a few more announcements, and you can get started with your day. Item One: a crew from HBO will be hanging around the school this semester, filming a new documentary called, "Scared Smart." They should be treated with appropriate courtesy and respect at all times. Anyone who embarrasses the school can expect a lengthy visit from Mr. Franklin.

SFX: LOUD BUZZING

[PRINCIPAL SNIFFS THE AIR.]

PRINCIPAL:

Mmm, bacon. Anyway, item two: Some of you have complained about the removal of the Suggestions Box outside my office. The reason is this: while your faith in democracy is impressive, the library isn't getting a subscription to High Times. Period.

Item Three: All music and arts instruction have been suspended until further notice, due to lack of funding. So if you want to learn any of that, you'll just have to pick it up on the streets.

Item Four: the first week of our Locker Search/Gun Buyback program has made over $7,000 for the school. This money will be placed in a fund and used to hire bounty hunters..

Finally, it has been brought to my attention that there is a website featuring supposedly nude pictures of me, running off a server in Tijuana. I have examined these photos and can say with certainty: that is not me. My head has been placed on a obese person's body. I have contacted the Mexican government and they assure me that the site will be coming down shortly.

Thanks to our conversations, I am picking up a little Spanish. Right now, my favorite phrase is "El Ben Franklin Special."

SFX: EXTREMELY LOUD BUZZING

SFX: APPLAUSE

OUT. □

GEORGE J. TENET

c/o Central Intelligence Agency
Langley, VA 23665 • 703 482-0623 • dci@cia.gov
(until 7/11/04; after: georgedaspook1@hotmail.com)

OBJECTIVE:

A challenging executive position that allows me to build upon my proven track record of success.

EXPERIENCE:

Director, Central Intelligence Agency
I have spent the last seven years heading the CIA, a large governmental agency charged with keeping secrets, gathering intelligence, and protecting the American People.

ACHIEVEMENTS:

Oversaw effort to pass classified information to Iran via Ahmed Chalabi, an obvious con-man, in hopes that Iranians would believe exact opposite. *(2004)*

Collected and analyzed vast amounts of information, so that it could be more effectively ignored by two Presidents. Spearheaded effort to streamline process by ignoring it within Agency. This program resulted in a catastrophic terrorist attack containing many very valuable lessons. *(1997-2004)*

Expanded clandestine operations, except in those countries unfriendly to US. *(1997-2004)*

Reorganized CIA after 40+ years of misinterpreting the Soviet Union; now possible to misinterpret 21st Century threats. *(1997-2004)*

Provided intelligence to expedite pre-planned invasion and occupation of Iraq. *(2003)*

Facilitated bombing of Chinese Embassy in Belgrade, improving relations with US' largest trading partner. *(1999)*

Provided intelligence for US' forces smashing victory against aspirin factory, setting back powerful Sudanese pharmaceutical industry.*(1998)*

Ignored Indian nuclear testing, allowing new arms race to blossom, and providing exotic locales for next generation of spy movies and novels. *(1998)*

SKILLS:

Can raise morale without evidence of competence
Professional manner that interfaces well with Senate investigations
Some knowledge of Word Perfect
Will take fall, if necessary

**DECLASSIFIED REFERENCES
AVAILABLE UPON REQUEST**

Assessing Ronald Reagan

Everybody knows that Ronald Reagan was singlehandedly responsible for the collapse of Communism and the end of the Cold War. That's obvious, and anybody who denies it is blinded by their own partisan hate. Of course he did it—it happened on his watch.

But the more important question, the one that all the eulogies dodge, is this: was Reagan a truly great man? To find this out, we must remember what else Reagan did while in office.

Mike & Jon
2004

In 1981 President Reagan...

...caused severe earthquakes in Peru, Iran, and Pakistan.
...produced a cable-tv version of Penthouse.
...made the Chinese a force in international competitive bridge.
...discovered monkeys in Kenya which use a rudimentary language.
...dug the world's largest hole, about 35,500 ft. deep.
...killed Hoagy Carmichael, the 82-year-old composer of "Stardust."

In 1982 President Reagan...

...led violent disorders in Miami, over the shooting of a black man by police.
...threw Sophia Loren in jail for 17 days for tax fraud.
...killed Leonid Brezhnev, leader of the Soviet Union.
...caused the longest lunar eclipse since 1736.
...beat the Milwaukee Brewers 4 games to 3, to clinch the World Series.

In 1983, President Reagan...

...celebrated the 100th anniversary of the Metropolitan Opera by spending eight hours singing selections from over 40 operas.
...awarded the Nobel Prize for Literature to William Golding.
...whipped through southern Texas, leaving 17 dead and causing $1.3 billion in damage.

In 1984, President Reagan...

...killed Yuri Andropov, leader of the Soviet Union.
...agreed to return Hong Kong to China in 1997.
...won eight Grammy awards, on his way to the biggest-selling album of all time.
...released toxic chemicals into the air over Bhopal, India, killing over 3500 people.
...became the first woman to walk in space.

In 1985, President Reagan...

...installed Mikhail Gorbachev as Chairman of the Communist Party of the USSR.
...won his third Tony award, for "Biloxi Blues."
...clashed with Italian soccer fans, killing 38.
...introduced tampons to China.

In 1986, President Reagan...

...exploded the Challenger, in America's worst space disaster.
...urged the use of condoms and abstinence to prevent the spread of AIDS.
...elected Jacques Chirac Prime Minister of France.
...circled the globe without refueling.

In 1987, President Reagan...

...landed a small plane in Red Square, and was sentenced to four years in a Soviet labor camp.
...won best film at Cannes for *Under Satan's Sun.*
...took four straight races from Australia's Kookaburra III, winning back the America's Cup.

In 1988, President Reagan...

...laid the first fiber-optic cable across the floor of the Atlantic.
...marked the centenary of Britain's notorious "Jack the Ripper."
...declared a new Soviet policy of "glasnost," or "openness."

In 1989, President Reagan...

...tore down the Berlin Wall, ending the Cold War.

What a man! Clearly Reagan was a restless polymath possessed of Herculean energy, always struggling to achieve , but like the rest of us, never quite sure of the outcome of his actions. Was Ronald Reagan a great man? Yes, we think so. No doubt about it. □

This Humor Piece: The Special Edition DVD

Mike & Jon
2003

"This Humor Piece plunges the reader into a 750-word maelstrom of nouns, punctuation, and synecdoche"—*Roger Ebert At the Humor Pieces*

Hailed upon its release as "the only humor piece of 2001 that really *matters*" (J. Hoberman, *Village Voice*), This Humor Piece tells a timeless story of analogies (Kevin Spacey) fighting to be drawn and the struggle of premises (Cameron Diaz) to extend themselves to their logical conclusion (Robin Williams) and beyond (Jim Carrey). Now available on DVD, this piece is sure to be treasured for generations.

THIS HUMOR PIECE: The Special Edition DVD ($28.99) includes:
- Instant access to all 17 paragraphs;
- Letterboxing to preserve the original aspect ratio;
- Subtitles in English, French, Kurdish, and Tagalog;
- Over 250 words not included in the original release;
- The uncut, uncensored video of This Humor Piece's smash hit title song, "Gonna Make You Laugh," performed by Sisquó;
- A 23-minute documentary, "Funny Business: The Making of This Humor Piece," featuring interviews with the piece's authors, editors, and typographers, giving you the inside story of its long, troubled road to publication.

THIS HUMOR PIECE: The Collector's Edition DVD ($42.99) includes all the above, plus:
- The infamous "spider walk" sequence, deemed too grisly for *The Atlantic;*

- "Laughing Matters," Spike Jonze's intimate look at the exhaustive, two year-long storyboarding process that took place on three continents—before the first word was ever written;
- A still photo gallery taken on location by Helmut Newton, featuring never-before-seen shots of the authors at work and play;
- Links and access codes to the piece's home on the Web, featuring chat rooms, a fast-paced trivia game, and a virtual reality preview of "This Humor Piece: The Ride" now under construction at Universal Studios Theme Park in Orlando, FL.

THIS HUMOR PIECE: The Deluxe 0th Anniversary Edition DVD ($99.99) includes all the above, plus:

- A comma-shaped, homeopathic DVD—the first of its kind to be approved by the U.S. Food and Drug Administration;
- The Director's Cut, featuring the entire 34,000 word original draft;
- A three-pound, gold-embossed, archival-quality display box;
- The long-suppressed soundtrack by master composer Nino Rota;
- The Dada-inspired original ending, which incited a Akron test-audience to riot;
- Two full-length audio commentaries featuring (1) the authors' ongoing argument about sentence 56, which devolves into tear-filled screaming, and (2) a sort of wavery, tuneless humming (a by-product, we think, of the bleeding-edge homeopathic printing process);
- "They CAN Smell Fear," a video profile of Arlene Schumann, the piece's legendary adverb wrangler;
- A "Guide to Proper Use of the Semi-Colon" limited edition collector's plate;
- Hilarious outtakes—from other things—featuring Burt Reynolds, Dom DeLuise, and Loni Anderson;
- The theatrical trailer for the upcoming This Humor Piece II: A New Beginning.

WARNING: For sale or rental for private home use in the USA and Canada only. Federal law provides severe civil and criminal penalties for unauthorized retelling of jokes without attribution. "Dolby" is a registered trademark of Dolby Laboratories Corp. "Humor" is a registered trademark of the Microsoft Corporation. ☐

OPPOSITE
Mike
2004

Last week, a convention of men and women certified to perform circumcisions met in a suburb of Washington, DC to discuss their trade. According to the hotel staff, they were all "tiny tippers."

Jon
Weekend Update
1998

Julia Roberts will be paid 17 million dollars for an upcoming movie that reunites her with Richard Gere. Meanwhile, all the girls who came to LA after seeing Pretty Woman will continue to be paid a hundred bucks per guy.

Jon
Weekend Update
1998

Foot rub turns non-sexual in wake of foot smell

Special to mikegerber.com

STUTTSTOWN, CT.—A potentially successful romantic encounter between two Stutts College students was derailed yesterday, after the sudden appearance of a noxious odor.

"It happened right after she took off her shoes, so I assume it came from her feet," said David Swanson, a junior. Though he has two younger sisters, both of whom are active in athletics, "I had no idea girls' feet could smell like that," Swanson said. "Shit, I didn't know a human being could produce that kind of stench and still be alive."

As of press time Swanson's companion, Jennifer Charbonneau, a sophomore majoring in History, was apparently unaware that any incident took place.

But Swanson remembers it well; he characterized the smell as "kinda fermenty, like rotten cheese or skunked beer, but with a little puke or something in there, too. God, I'm gagging just describing it." Along with the raw power of the emanation, the Econ major was also impressed by the odor's almost-supernatural staying power. "I could still smell it for at least an hour after Jen left. I had to wash the cover on my futon."

The doomed pair had met in Swanson's room in Rascomb Hall to study for a Chem test, he said. "We did that for a while, then decided to take a study break. I got out some Bailey's that my ex-girlfriend had forgotten to take, and one thing led to another."

Friends say that foot rubbing is a common seduction strategy for Swanson, who is renowned for his skill. "Once the shoes come off, the pants are soon to follow," said a friend.

Swanson says he had a couple of beers before Jen arrived. "The guy across the hall offered 'em to me, and I was a little nervous." Charbonneau, assistant Treasurer of the Omicron Gamma sorority, is considered to be quite popular and attractive. "Anyway, I learn better with a buzz on," said Swanson, "but as soon as the smell hit, I was stone cold sober."

The massage that followed was extremely perfunctory, as Swanson blinked back tears and fought not to cough. "For such a cute little person, she sure makes a big, horrible stink."

Charbonneau noticed the change in Swanson's behavior, but says she has no idea what caused it. "All of the sudden, Dave got weird, like he wanted me to hurry up and leave," she said. "He certainly wasn't acting that way before. Then, out of nowhere, he was 'really tired.' I'm like, 'Dude, you need meds.'"

"It was like she didn't even smell it," Swanson said. "Maybe she's used to it, or has something like color-blindness, but for feet."

According to medical records, Charbonneau wears orthotics, devices worn inside the shoe to correct problems with walking, running or other foot-related activities. "I've been meaning to throw them in the washer, but I always forget," she said. "Why do you ask?"

For Swanson, hard feelings remain. "I don't want to be an asshole or anything," he said, "but I told my friends—for their own protection." Swanson feels bad, but believes that "somebody has to tell her eventually—otherwise, what kind of life will she have? I just hope it isn't me."

Swanson isn't looking forward to their Chemistry class, which has ten weeks to go. "It's going to be awkward," he said. "I hope she doesn't sit next to me. Too many bad memories."

Sketch: "The Smithsonian"

Jon
WNYC
2001

HOST

Lawrence Small hasn't been making a whole lot of friends since he took over as head of the Smithsonian Institution, thanks in part to his willingness to take donations from people like Catherine Reynolds. Reynolds gave the Smithsonian $38 million to build a "Hall of Fame of American Achievers," featuring the 100 greatest achievers in U.S. history, in exchange for picking two-thirds of the committee who decides who's chosen. Ms. Reynolds has already recommended Oprah Winfrey, Martha Stewart, Dorothy Hamill, Sam Donaldson, and Frederick Smith, the founder of Federal Express.

(phone rings)

REYNOLDS

Hello.

SMALL

Catherine! It's Larry!

REYNOLDS

Larry...?

SMALL

Larry Small!

REYNOLDS

Ah, the towel boy from the club. Have you found my bracelet yet?

SMALL

No, no, Larry Small -- from the Smithsonian!

REYNOLDS

Oh! Right, right, we gave you a little bit of money.

SMALL

That's right -- $38 million for the Hall of Fame of American Achievers. I just wanted to call to reiterate that we're very excited -- incredibly excited! -- about working with you on this. The second thing, and I even hate to mention this, is I was looking over your list of the top 100 achievers, and I just had a few questions.

REYNOLDS

Um-hmm.

SMALL

I see #1 and 2 are Oprah Winfrey and Martha Stewart.

REYNOLDS

Yes, it was so hard to decide who should be #1. But then I thought, well, Oprah has been on longer.

SMALL

And then #3 is Terry Bradshaw.

REYNOLDS

That's right!

SMALL

...Terry Bradshaw, the old quarterback for the Pittburgh Steelers?

REYNOLDS

Was he? I just know he does those funny little commercials for 10-10-220.

SMALL

I see. And then, as I read it, #6 is "Deepak Chopra and Regis Philbin."

REYNOLDS

Yes.

SMALL

So achiever #6 is TWO people.

REYNOLDS

Yes.

SMALL

And that would explain #9, "The Cast of Ally McBeal."

REYNOLDS

Yes, I don't know their names, but they're just so clever!

SMALL

Then...I wasn't familiar with numbers 22 through 54, but I did notice that all their last names were, uh, Reynolds.

REYNOLDS

Right, that's my mother, and sisters, and cousins. I just knew if I left anyone off, well, no more Christmas cards for me!

SMALL

And #48, "Mr. Merrybells Reynolds." He's your brother...?

REYNOLDS

No, no, he's my new Akita puppy! Oh, he's so cute. He's being housebroken, and I thought Mr. Merrybells needed some positive reinforcement.

SMALL

Okay. I guess my last question is #92, "Jean-Luc Picard."

REYNOLDS

That's right! "To boldly go when no one has gone before!"

SMALL

Yes. He's sort of a hard one for us, because not only is he not America, he's not...a real person.

REYNOLDS

But he's so sexy!

SMALL

He is! He is sexy! So...he would be a great choice if we were doing a Hall of Sexy Made Up Foreigners. But this is a Hall of Fame of American Achievers.

REYNOLDS

I don't see your point, Mr. Smalls. Is this the way you treat all your customers?

SMALL

(LICKSPITTLEISH) That's why I thought we should have this little talk. To me, these are all WONDERFUL examples of American Achievement, every last one. If it were just me I'd said, "Go for it! Put it up! Be inspired, America!" But it's not just me. At the Smithsonian we have all these -- well, they call themselves "scholars."

REYNOLDS

Oh, scholars! What do THEY know about anything?

SMALL

My thoughts exactly. So I wanted to tell you about an exciting new opportunity we have for donors. Basically, this is an opportunity for you to...give us more money. In the past donors could give for general support or a particular exhibit, but now we allow them to donate in much more targeted personal ways.

REYNOLDS

Ooooh.

SMALL

For instance, the government refuses to pay for my car and driver. Coca-Cola has donated for that...which is why none of our museums now have water fountains.

REYNOLDS

So I ask you: what would it take for Jean-Luc to make it into the Hall of Fame?

SMALL

Frankly, dealing with the hoi polloi makes me tense. Very tense. To function at the highest level, which you might call a "Captain of the Enterprise Level," I'm really going to need a vacation home...in Sri Lanka.

REYNOLDS

Well...Number One, make it so! ☐

If H.P. Lovecraft and P.G. Wodehouse Were the Same Person

Mike
Fall 2001

I.

"It is a known fact of veterinary science," said Lord Boggleton, settling in to his favorite topic, "that cats must be fed mayonnaise thrice daily. Anyone who disagrees is a fool."

"What if they don't like it?" asked his guest, Catherine Tramway. She was the visiting widow of an American ball-bearing magnate, and a strong candidate to take this moldering old pile off the family's hands at a handsome profit. "Surely you don't force them?"

Bill winced inwardly. Sensing the sale--or, more to the point, his commission--slipping away, he quickly soothed Mrs. Tramway's sensibilities. "No, no, of course not."

Boggleton was immediately incensed. "That's ridiculous! My dear woman, you mustn't coddle your felines! A few lashes with a very small whip--"

Colonel Brabazon charged in, all moustache and bluster and muscle gone to fat. Bill said a silent prayer of thanks for the interruption.

"I found this book in the library!" he exclaimed.

"Imagine that," said Bill's wife Monica.

"It looks dashed old." The Colonel had been stationed in Egypt, so he considered himself a bit of an expert on antiquity. They all gathered around.

"The *Necronomicon*?" Monica asked. "What does that mean?"

"Latin, I imagine," said the Colonel. "Or Greek."

"It is Arabic in origin," said Peeves, with a queer gleam in his eye. "The work of one Abdul Alhazred, also known as 'the mad Arab.'"

"What is its opinion on the subject of cats?" Lord Boggleton said.

"Only one way to find out," said Mrs. Tramway brightly. Like many rich woman, she was allergic to waiting, and opened the book.

"Tally-ho," muttered Peeves, and slipped away.

II.

After reading a few gruesome, blasphemous passages, the party was collectively tottering on the brink of cosmic horrors beyond man's ability to bear. Still, for the Colonel at least, a shred of lip-stiffness remained. The Code, he thought, the Code. What would Bascombe or Squiffy think if I quailed in front of a book?

"I say, Lord Boggleton, I may be tottering on the brink of cosmic horrors and all that rot, but it seems bloody strange, you having such a book."

"I am as flummoxed as you are, Colonel Brabazon," their host replied. "Peeves must have unearthed it while reorganizing the Library.

"What's that noise?" said Bill, walking toward the open window. Muffled tom-toms could be heard. "There appears to be some sort of commotion in the vicinity of the lake."

"It's those RSPCA blighters again!" said Lord Boggleton, naming his bete noire.

"Let's go have a look," Monica said, and the rest followed.

The oft-surly and unpredictable English summer smiled upon the group as they crossed the sunny lawn into the copse. Once inside, however, they were confronted by willows contorted as if by torture, malignant nooses of Spanish moss, lichens arranged in patterns of decay and foreboding. Along the once-pleasant path there hung a palpable sense of unnamable evil.

"The garden seems to have rather gone to pot," Bill said, then caught himself. "but it's nothing a good landscaper couldn't fix."

"No use in being sentimental, I must sack that McTavish," Boggleton grumbled, plucking at a monstrous fern that seemed to suck ravenously at his shoe.

They rounded the bend, and saw a blood-chilling sight: At the water's edge were clustered all the meanest inhabitants of nearby Lower Boggleton. Members of the household staff led the orgiastic proceedings, chief among them none other than Peeves.

"Rather a lot of half-caste cult fiends for a sleepy English village, don't you think?" Monica said.

"Still, it takes all kinds!" Bill said, solely for Mrs. Tramway's benefit.

"McTavish, I want a word with you!" Lord Boggleton yelled. The gardener made no reply, concentrating instead on his arcane chanting and spasms.

The nightmare corpse-city of R'yleh had risen up in the middle of the lake, its ooze-covered bulk obscuring the gently rolling hills beyond. Its vast, awesome, and incalculable age cut no ice with the property's owner. "That wasn't there yesterday," he said. "It's a blamed eyesore."

Wafting above this eerie scene was the unholy chanting of McTavish and the others: "Ph'nglui mglw'nafh Cthulhu R'lyeh wgah'nagl fhtagn!'

"What does that mean?" asked Monica.

"Something to the effect of, 'This Cthulu blighter is utterly top-hole,' I expect, " said the Colonel. "I encountered some of these chaps in a watering-hole in Singapore," he said. "They asked me for a donation."

"I bloody well hope you gave them one!" Bill shouted, his nerves shot. There went the sale, he thought. Who would want to live near a corpse-city and a chorus of bellowing lunatics?

Mrs. Tramway suddenly screamed, and all attention was focused on her. "I've lost my diamond necklace!"

A collective gasp riffled the now-brackish water. "But who could've taken it?" Bill asked.

"Well, as much as it pains me to accuse somebody not present to defend himself," said the Colonel, "my money's on this C'thulu chap."

III.

A slight rustling could be heard immediately to their left. Was it that foul deity which the crustaceans of Yuggoth worship as the Nether-One, and which the vaporous brains of the spiral nebulae know by an untranslatable sign? No, it was only Archie Boggleton, the Lord's spendthrift youngest son, down from Cambridge and irritating everyone with a power beyond his years.

He bounded into the group, apparently insensible to the horrors that lurk ceaselessly behind time and space.

"Ripping day, what?" The activity at the lake then caught his attention. "Pardon me, but who the deuce are all those chaps? Is that the cook?" Archie tried to cast himself as a paragon of decorum. "That's not very proper, is it? Dancing naked and bloody and what?" Lord Boggleton, unconvinced by the performance, fixed Archie with a gimlet eye. Something was fishy, but whether it was another of Archie's money-making schemes, or horrifying blasphemies from an elder star, he couldn't say.

Suddenly, from the middle of the cursed, non-Euclidean city, an immense rune-covered door of carved rock split open. The blackness that oozed forth dissipated slowly into a gibbous sky. Then, amid wild applause from Peeves and his cronies, something horrible emerged. A pulpy, octopus-like head, its face a mass of feelers, squeezed through the portal, followed by a scaly, rubbery-looking, winged body. Soon three hundred feet of elder demon stood revealed in the unblinking sun.

"It's those blasted RSPCA!" Lord Boggleton immediately went mad, which, after all, wasn't that far a distance to go. The foul creature scooped him up and consumed him. A cheer issued from his ex-employees.

Summoning up the courage shown by his forebears at Crecy and Agincourt, Bill, the newly-minted Lord Boggleton, ran like hell. He was swept up by a massive scaly hand and disappeared into that tentacle-fringed mouth. Monica, catatonic with fright, followed.

Colonel Brabazon pulled out a small revolver, a momento of the Sudan, and began to fire. It was completely ineffectual.

As Archie was being hoisted up to the unholy god's all-consuming maw, a diamond necklace slipped from his pocket and fell to the ground. Mrs. Tramway made no response; her gaze was fixed on the great beast, a look of benign puzzlement on her face.

The claw swept down. "Wait, let me ask you," she said calmly. "You're not one of the Pittsburgh C'thulus, are you?"

The hellish visitor from beyond time and space beamed a "yes" into her puny brain.

"You didn't go by the nickname 'Kooky', did you?" The demon's tentacles arranged themselves into a smile. "Here you were killing everybody, and I thought, 'How many C'thulus could there possibly be?' We went to high school together, don't you remember? I was plain old Kathy Stevens back then."

On the bank, the demon's followers grew restive. "Eat her!" Peeves cried. "Eat her! Eat her! *Eat her!*"

"I had such a crush on you," the heiress said, blushing. "Still have, in fact."

Hundreds of feet above the relentlessly nattering American, C'thulu's heart leapt. Countless eons ago, he had gone away, fearing that such a woman would never marry somebody as penniless as he, even if he was a supremely powerful elder demon, the foulest excrescence of pure evil ever to exist on this or any other plane. But now...

"Could you ever love a —" he asked telepathically.

"Of course I could, you big lump. It's settled. We're getting married! You tell Yog-Sothoth, I'm calling the *Times!*" □

Monologue: "Locker Room Speech, November 22nd, 1963"

Mike & Jon
2003

[SCENE: A dingy locker room reeking of sweat, mildew, and disinfectant. A dejected group of football players, smeared with grass and blood sit in various postures of utter defeat. The COACH, a florid, beefy guy in a star-spangled windbreaker, strides to the middle of the room; after blowing his whistle to get everybody's attention, he speaks.]

COACH

All right, everybody! Listen up! Okay. Well, we had a rough day out there. We did some things wrong, and got some bad breaks. It's always tough when the quarterback gets shot in the head.

But teams have lost quarterbacks before. They got through it, and we're gonna get through it, too. Hell, some of 'em even made it to the Super Bowl, and if Lyndon plays like we all expect him to, we just might do that! But that's not what I'm worried about. What I'm worried about is us staying together as a team.

'Cause I'm telling you, it's already happening. People—reporters, the knuckleheads on sports radio—they're already starting with the questions, like, "Who the frig shot the quarterback?" And, "Why the frig did they shoot the quarterback?" And, "How the frig can we keep the quarterback from getting shot again?"

But you know what, gentlemen? That doesn't matter. It doesn't—friggin'—matter. What matters is next week's game, not what happened this week. So I suggest you all just put it out of your mind, and move on. 'Cause in this game, teams that live in the past, lose. Look at France.

Take a look around this room. These people are the only ones whose opinion matters a good goddamn. If you don't stick together, we won't have a chance, not next Sunday, or the one after that, or ever. We succeed together, or we don't succeed at all. So everybody in this room—listen up, Malcolm—you gotta decide: which friggin' side am I on? Am I on the team's side, or am I on the side of the nobodies sitting in the cheap seats? Martin, Bobby—shut the frig up and listen.

If you guys stick together, I'm gonna make you a promise: nobody's gonna get cut from the team. Everybody did their goddamn level best out there—J. Edgar, you Dulles boys, I saw you busting your asses—and I'm not planning on making any changes. Sometimes things just happen, and if you start turning a team upside-down just because the quarterback gets shot in the head, you're screwed.

'Cause we're not in charge of Results, gentlemen. That's not our Department. Our Department is Effort, that's our Department. Somebody getting shot in the head, that's a Result. Only one guy is in the Results Department, and that's God.

Here's the hard truth: Next week somebody else may get shot. Maybe Malcolm'll get shot. And then two weeks after that, maybe Martin will get shot in the face or something. I don't know, it might happen. It's possible. And then maybe Bobby'll get shot in the same friggin' game!

My point is, you don't know. That's just the way this game is. People are going to get shot. And as much as the reporters and fans and all the people who've never played a goddamn minute of football in their lives bitch and moan, there's no point in asking "Why?" or "Who let the quarterback ride in an open motorcade?" or "Can't you see that if you don't get to the bottom of this, sooner or later the fans will lose faith in the team and get pissed off, and maybe not even show up?" Now, that's one thing I'm not worried about—the fans'll come. They gotta come. What other choice do they have, not voting? What do you think would happen if we did whatever the fans told us to? It'd be anarchy, that's what would happen. Plus, we'd all be out of jobs!

So, starting at practice tomorrow, we're gonna all pretend like this didn't happen. We're not gonna study film—we all saw it, we don't need friggin' Zapruder to remind us. We're just gonna start preparing for next week. Moving on.

That's what Jack would want. Do you think he cares who shot him? No! Not where he is now. And we shouldn't either... Now, shower up and we'll get 'em next week. Right? I can't hear you, ladies! RIGHT? □

Another book proposal (1996). Usually they said the target wasn't big enough, This time, they said the market would be glutted with parodies.

It wasn't, of course. Thank god for self-publishing.

Harry Potter and the Errant Golf Cart

Mike & Jon
The New York Times
July 2003

In today's cynical world, where things seldom justify their hype, we're happy to report the following: *Harry Potter and the Order of the Phoenix* rocks!

J. K. Rowling has really outdone herself. Harry, Ron and Hermione are in fine form, and the plot has plenty of surprises. The whole Voldemort-has-weapons-of-mass-destruction subplot, for example—touching and timely. And who would've expected an overview of the conceptual art of Yoko Ono, right there in Chapter 19? I mean, it's Ms. Rowling's book, she can write what she wants, but that's one development we did not see coming. (We'll have to reread *Goblet of Fire* to make sure.)

Of course, with two Pottermaniacs as devoted as we are, chances were good we would like "Phoenix," no matter what. How devoted are we? How many people actually quit their jobs so they will have more time to read it? (The guy at the unemployment office said, "I admire what you two are doing"—he didn't have to say that.) All summer, with nothing to do but read Book Five...who's laughing now, suckers? By suckers, we mean our parents, our wives, the mortgage company, and so forth.

Many people scoffed at our months-long preparation for the release of *Phoenix*. "New glasses, O.K.," the judge said. "Building a special 'Potterbunker' with six months of provisions and a chemical toilet? Fine, it's your money. But quitting work? Severing contact with your families? Isn't that a little excessive?"

"I guess making little wizard hats for the cats to wear is 'excessive,' too!" we told him, defiantly. "I suppose crashing a golf cart into the bookstore window, creating a diversion that would ensure we got the first copies, is 'excessive.' If that's 'excessive,' we don't want to be 'cessive,' your honor!"

You have to understand the kind of pressure we were under. We had been jumpy for weeks, knowing that the books were in warehouses nearby, yet we couldn't get at them. Copies were under armed guard, and the buildup was relentless.

You couldn't escape it. The conflict between Harry and Voldemort is too sweeping, too elemental, too lucrative to be contained in mere books. It has spawned everything from movies to toothpaste. In this environment, it was only a matter of time before we snapped. (Besides, if you publish a book 870 pages long, you have to expect that sooner or later someone's going to use it as a weapon.)

But now we have *Phoenix*, and all's right with the world. Granted, our impressions of it are a bit hazy—between rereading the first four books, getting in line early Wednesday, then deciding instead to do the thing with the golf cart, running from the mob, being trapped in the burning windmill, the cops, the arraignment—what we're trying to say is, we haven't slept in 168 hours, so you'd better read it for yourself.

While we're waiting to be sentenced, we'd like to thank J. K. Rowling for bringing so much excitement into our lives. Thank you, Ms. Rowling, and thank you, Harry. We'll be reading and enjoying *Order of the Phoenix* for many years to come. (Most likely three to five years, according to our lawyer.) □

www.ingramcontent.com/pod-product-compliance
Lightning Source LLC
LaVergne TN
LVHW080924110826
845155LV00039B/205

* 9 7 8 1 8 9 0 4 7 0 0 4 3 *